LITERARY CRITICISM AND CULTURAL THEORY

OUTSTANDING DISSERTATIONS

edited by

William E. Cain

Wellesley College

A ROUTLEDGE SERIES

OTHER BOOKS IN THIS
SERIES:

A COINCIDENCE OF WANTS
The Novel and Neoclassical Economics
Charles Lewis

MODERN PRIMITIVES
*Race and Language in Gertrude Stein, Ernest
Hemingway, and Zora Neale Hurston*
Susanna Pavloska

PLAIN AND UGLY JANES
*The Rise of the Ugly Woman in Contemporary
American Fiction*
Charlotte M. Wright

DISSENTING FICTIONS
*Identity and Resistance in the Contemporary
American Novel*
Cathy Moses

PERFORMING LA MESTIZA
*Textual References of Lesbians of Color and the
Negotiation of Identities*
Ellen M. Gil-Gomez

FROM GOOD MA TO WELFARE QUEEN
*A Genealogy of the Poor Woman in American
Literature, Photography and Culture*
Vivyan C. Adair

ARTFUL ITINERARIES
*European Art and American Careers in High
Culture, 1865–1920*
Paul Fisher

POSTMODERN TALES OF SLAVERY
IN THE AMERICAS
From Alejo Carpenter to Charles Johnson
Timothy J. Cox

EMBODYING BEAUTY
*Twentieth-Century American Women
Writers' Aesthetics*
Malin Pereira

MAKING HOMES IN THE WEST/INDIES
*Constructions of Subjectivity in the
Writings of Michelle Cliff and Jamaica Kincaid*
Antonia Macdonald-Smythe

POSTCOLONIAL MASQUERADES
*Culture and Politics in Literature, Film,
Video, and Photography*
Niki Sampat Patel

DIALECTIC OF SELF AND STORY
*Reading and Storytelling in Contemporary
American Fiction*
Robert Durante

ALLEGORIES OF VIOLENCE
*Tracing the Writings of War in Late
Twentieth-Century Fiction*
Lidia Yuknavitch

VOICE OF THE OPPRESSED IN THE LANGUAGE
OF THE OPPRESSOR
*A Discussion of Selected Postcolonial Literature
from Ireland, Africa and America*
Patsy J. Daniels

EUGENIC FANTASIES
*Racial Ideology in the Literature and Popular
Culture of the 1920's*
Betsy L. Nies

THE LIFE WRITING OF OTHERNESS
Woolf, Baldwin, Kingston, and Winterson
Lauren Rusk

"THOUGHTS PAINFULLY INTENSE"
Hawthorne and the Invalid Author
James N. Mancall

FROM WITHIN THE FRAME

Storytelling in African-American Fiction

Bertram D. Ashe

ROUTLEDGE
NEW YORK & LONDON

Published in 2002 by
Routledge
29 West 35th Street
New York, NY 10001
www.Routledge-NY.com

Published in Great Britain by
Routledge
11 New Fetter Lane
London EC4P 4EE

Routledge is an imprint of the Taylor & Francis Group.

10 9 8 7 6 5 4 3 2 1

Library of Congress Cataloging-in-Publication

Ashe, Bertram D., 1959–
    From within the frame : storytelling in African-American fiction / by Bertram D. Ashe.
        p. cm. — (Literary criticism and cultural theory)
    Includes bibliographical references and index.
    ISBN 0-415-93954-2 (acid-free paper)
    1. American fiction—African American authors—History and criticism. 2. American
fiction—20th century—History and criticism. 3. Frame-stories—History and criticism.
4. African Americans in literature. 5. Storytelling in literature. I. Title. II. Series.
    PS374.N4 A84 2002
    813.009'23'08996073--dc21

                                                                                    2002002524

Printed on acid-free, 250 year-life paper
Manufactured in the United States of America

For my family,
Dr. Bertram L. Ashe, Dolly Ashe, David Ashe and
Dr. Pamela Ashe-Thomas:
thanks for setting the bar so high

For Jordan,
who crawled, then walked, then ran
into my home office as pages became chapters

For Garnet
(who also has a peculiar connection to my office),
who appeared mid-way through
and immediately elbowed himself onto these pages

and most of all:

for Valerie

whose love (and patience)
made it all worthwhile

Contents

ACKNOWLEDGMENTS   *ix*

INTRODUCTION   1

CHAPTER 1
"A little personal attention":
Storytelling and the Black Audience in
Charles W. Chesnutt's *The Conjure Woman*   9

CHAPTER 2
"Ah don't mean to bother wid tellin' 'em nothin'":
Zora Neale Hurston's Critique of the Storytelling
Aesthetic in *Their Eyes Were Watching God*   29

CHAPTER 3
Listening to the Blues: Ralph Ellison's Trueblood
Episode in *Invisible Man*   47

CHAPTER 4
The Best "Possible Returns":
Storytelling and Gender Relations in
James Alan McPherson's "The Story of a Scar"   61

CHAPTER 5
From Within the Frame:
Narrative Negotiations with the Black Aesthetic in
Toni Cade Bambara's "My Man Bovanne"   77

CHAPTER 6
"Would she have believed any of it?":
Interrogating the Storytelling Motive in
John Edgar Wideman's "Doc's Story"   93

NOTES   109

BIBLIOGRAPHY   133

INDEX   143

Acknowledgments

I would like to express my appreciation to Professors Joanne Braxton, Jacquelyn McLendon, Arthur Knight, H. Cam Walker, and, especially, Susan Donaldson for their careful reading and criticism of the manuscript.

I would like to thank Professor Robert Gross, the College of William and Mary American Studies program, and Jean Brown, who greatly helped the author toward completion. A William and Mary Summer Research Fellowship funded research on Charles Chesnutt at Fisk University.

I'm grateful to Professor Ray Hilliard, chair, and the English department at the University of Richmond for the use of office space and library privileges during the summer following my visiting instructorship.

Karen Veselits, Renee Sentilles, Marland Buckner, Colleen Doyle Worrell, and Crystal Anderson are only a few of my friends and supporters who were there to critique, commiserate and celebrate the steps toward completion of the manuscript. Thanks, also, to Daryl Cumber Dance, Professor of English at the University of Richmond, and John Callahan, Morgan S. Odell Professor of Humanities at Lewis and Clark College, for valuable advice. Thanks, as well, to my English department colleagues at the College of the Holy Cross.

Finally, I would like to thank Professor Robert Burns Stepto, Professor of English and African American and American Studies at Yale University, for providing such compelling scholarship on storytelling in African-American fiction, for agreeing to lend his valuable time to reading and commenting on the manuscript, and for not minding that the title of my project is a presumptuous but respectful reference to his landmark study of African-American narrative.

FROM WITHIN THE FRAME

Introduction

For us African-Americanists perhaps the most significant aspect of the idea of *lieux de mémoire* ["sites of memory"] was its capacity to suggest new categories of sources for the historian: new sets of sometimes very difficult readings. We considered, for example, how to read certain dances, paintings, buildings, journals, and oral forms of expression. More than ever, we saw novels, poems, slave narratives, autobiographies, and oral testimonies as crucial parts of the historical record. These varied repositories of individual memories, taken together, create a collective communal memory.[1]

> –Geneviéve Fabre and Robert G. O'Meally,
> *History and Memory in African-American Culture*

Charles Waddell Chesnutt's "The Goophered Grapevine" first appeared in the *Atlantic Monthly* in 1887. John Edgar Wideman first published "Doc's Story" in *Esquire* magazine in 1986. Historically, the hundred years between Chesnutt's and Wideman's frame stories have contained a variety of issues that concern the written representation of African American spoken-voice storytelling. The use of an inside-the-text listener situates a storyteller–and that storyteller's story–within a particular reality and, as such, creates a vibrant, fluid storytelling event. Consciously or unconsciously, African-American writers periodically use a narrative frame as a medium for negotiation with their readership; the inside-the-text listeners, argues Walter Ong below, mirror their anticipated readers. These narrative negotiations vary in audience, form and content, but the frame tale convention, in one way or another, speaks to the reader as well as the listener, in each.

This study of written African-American oral storytelling grows out of projects such as Geneviéve Fabre and Robert O'Meally's, particularly as I study the literary storytelling *event*, the interaction between author, teller, listening audience and reading audience. "As a group looking at these complex forms of expression," writes Fabre and O'Meally, "we realized our responsibility to confront the issue of audience: of those directly and indirectly addressed by these varied historical makers and markers, these *lieux de mémoire*" (9).

Oral storytelling is, after all, intimately concerned with audience. A typical "frame" text is a novel or story in which the opening paragraphs of the text contextualize a coming tale, providing the reader with the setting, the narrator, the teller, and the listener, who is often the narrator. This section of a frame text is called the "open frame," which begins the story or novel. The open frame ends when the tale begins, and in most frame texts the tale is rendered virtually uninterrupted until completed. When the tale is over, the narrator/listener regains (explicit) control of the narrative, so that once again the reader sees the action of the story through the listener or narrator's point-of-view. (Occasionally there is no close frame at all.) Taken together, the open and close frame act as a mediator between the tale and the reader. In much the same way a traditional frame around a painting controls the viewer's visual movement from wall to painting back to wall,[2] the open and close frames in a frame text prevent the teller from speaking "directly" to the reader. In a frame text, the teller is "speaking" to the inside-the-text "listener"; the listener/narrator, in turn, "speaks" to the reader. The conversation that results is a form of call-and-response, an aspect of the African-American vernacular tradition.[3]

But the frame text, whether it is a novel such as Joseph Conrad's *Heart of Darkness* or Mary Shelley's *Frankenstein*, or a short story by Thomas Nelson Page, Mark Twain, or Joel Chandler Harris, is not the only way fiction writers represent oral storytelling. The "embedded narrative" is another form of teller-listener-reader communication. While the frame text has, in most cases, explicit and identifiable frames to open and close the narrative at large, embedded narratives, on the other hand, are storytelling events that momentarily occur in short stories or novels as the narrative marches forward. Although these embedded narratives are important to the whole, structurally they are not central to the text–if they were, they would be formal frame texts.[4]

Nevertheless, tellers whose tales are "embedded" rather than "framed" do influence the text and are vital in their own way; they do, after all, have inside-the-text audiences. Perhaps most importantly, the lack of strict open and close frames in novels or stories that contain embedded narratives allow the teller-listener-reader relationship to have consequences over a longer range of narrative time (a storytelling event early in the narrative can play a critical plot- and theme-twisting role late in the narrative, as we shall see in Ralph Ellison's *Invisible Man*). The embedded narrative, then, brings its own advantages to the written representation of spoken-voice storytelling.

But to what, exactly, does the term "African-American spoken voice" refer? There are several ways to address the nettlesome problem of identifying a black spoken voice. It is difficult to tell the difference between a voice meant to be "read" and a voice meant to be "heard." The problem is solved easily enough in a text like James Weldon Johnson's *The Autobiography of an Ex-Coloured Man*, which begins, "I know that in writing the following pages I am divulging the great secret of my life. . . ."[5] The novel is rendered in first-person, but makes conscious references to being written, and therefore is meant to be "read." Similarly, Ralph Ellison's Invisible Man, in his epilogue, writes, "So why do I write, torturing myself to put it all down?"[6]

Conversely, it should be assumed that if a narrative refers to being "heard," then someone is talking. In Gloria Naylor's *Mama Day*, for example, Cocoa says, "I sound awful, don't I? Well, those were awful times in that city of yours. . . ."[7] The explicit reference to "sound" validates the orality of the narrator. Still other black spoken-voice narratives, such as Sherley Anne Williams's "Tell Martha Not To Moan," use an identifiable Black English dialect: "That really funny to em. They all cracking up but me. . . . And I know it like I say; any woman can give a man money."[8] (*Norton Anthology*). As Geneva Smitherman writes in *Talkin and Testifyin*, "Black Dialect is an Africanized form of English reflecting Black America's linguistic cultural African heritage and the conditions of servitude, oppression, and life in America. Black Language is Euro-American speech with an Afro-American meaning, nuance, tone, and gesture."[9] Toni Cade Bambara's "My Man Bovanne" is another example of narrative rendered in Black English dialect. Cocoa, Naylor's narrator, does not speak Black English. But in this instance, her reference to being "heard" earmarks her speech as oral. And since she is an African-American character, she must possess an African-American spoken voice, even if that voice does not possess what Smitherman calls above the "linguistic cultural African heritage" that would aurally identify it as "black."

But what happens when an African-American first-person narrator is "speaking" in Standard English dialect and doesn't make pointed reference to the act of speaking? Although she argues against it, Smitherman acknowledges that "Some blacks try to solve the linguistic ambivalence dilemma by accepting certain features or types of black speech and rejecting others . . . [some] middle class blacks, for example, accept the black semantics of musicians and hipsters but reject the black syntax of working class blacks" (174). Reginald McKnight's narrator in "Mali Is Very Dangerous" is a good example. He speaks in Standard English dialect throughout the story: "I wasn't interested in M.D.'s 'sister,' but I was certainly intrigued. Maybe mystified would be a better word, for it seemed to me that M.D. was offering me the whore for nothing."[10] But McKnight's narrator nods to Smitherman in this passage, where he buys some Heineken for M.D. and his sister:

"Hinkin!" said M.D. "He bring us Hinkin. Oh, you very big man. You are as boss." Oh cripes, I thought. I am as fool. Rule number thirty-two for getting by in Senegal: *never try to buy yourself out of a pain in the ass.* M.D., steadily tapping my leg, giving me a sinner's grin, said, "You like my sister?" He said this the way Millie Jackson would say, "You like my sweet thang, don't you baby?" And for some reason still a mystery to me today, I said, "Yes-M.D.-I-really-like-your-sister-but-you-see-I-am-married." He looked at me as if I had said, "I-am-in-Senegal" and without blinking, twitching, flinching, said, "You like my sister?" (5)

McKnight's narrator informs his Standard English usage with a black idiolect. As a result, his narrator "sounds" like a black speaker, even though he isn't talking in Black English, and doesn't make an explicit reference to talking or being heard.

These are all examples of the African-American spoken voice. Most importantly, the black spoken voice is a voice that appears to want to be "heard" rather than "read," regardless of whether it leans toward Standard English or Black English. In this study, the texts I examine, whether formal frame texts or not, identify themselves as being rendered in black spoken-voice.[11]

Regardless of the nature of the spoken voice, the frame story form does cede what Robert Stepto calls "authorial control"[12] from the storyteller inside the frame to the listener/narrator. Or as Gayl Jones, talking specifically about Charles W. Chesnutt's *The Conjure Woman*, puts it, "[T]he question of authority is open; we're not sure really who controls the story."[13] At issue, for the most part, was the containment of black speech, largely for audience-related reasons. Certainly, there have long been periodic "frameless" black spoken-voice narratives, but Standard English-speaking narrators have more often "framed" black dialect storytellers throughout African-American literary history. As John Edgar Wideman writes in "Frame and Dialect: The Evolution of the Black Voice," "From the point of view of American literature then, the fact of black speech (and the oral roots of a distinct literary tradition–ultimately the tradition itself) existed only when it was properly 'framed,' within works which had status in the dominant literary system. For black speech the frame was the means of entering the literate culture in order to define the purposes or ends for which black speech could be employed."[14] *From Within the Frame* treats the struggle for authorial control in written oral storytelling in each of the three frame text forms: the formal frame text (in Charles Chesnutt's *The Conjure Woman*, Zora Neale Hurston's *Their Eyes Were Watching God*, James Alan McPherson's "The Story of a Scar," and Wideman's "Doc's Story"), the embedded narrative (*Invisible Man*, by Ralph Ellison), and the "frameless" storytelling event ("My Man Bovanne," by Toni Cade Bambara).

But there is still more at stake in the use of a narrative frame. Walter Ong has discussed the process of writers "fictionalizing" their audience. The practice of writing is, after all, essentially a solitary activity, one where, as opposed to the oral speech act, the audience must be imagined. As Ong writes, the writer "is writing. No one is listening. There is no feedback. Where does he find his 'audience'? He has to make his readers up, fictionalize them."[15] But according to Ong, while the writer must fictionalize his or her readers, the readership is simultaneously called upon to fictionalize themselves as receivers of the fiction:

> Readers over the ages have had to learn this game of literacy, how to conform themselves to the projections of the writers they read, or at least how to operate in terms of these projections. They have to know how to play the game of being a member of an audience that "really" does not exist. And they have to adjust when the rules change, even though no rules thus far have ever been published and even though the changes in the unpublished rules are themselves for the most part only implied. (61)

Certainly, Ong continues, "the roles readers are called on to play evolve without any explicit rules or directives" (62), but there are, indeed, examples of the *im*plicit rules alluded to in the block quotation above. Chancer's *Canterbury Tales* is his primary citation: By setting the stories within a frame, writes Ong, "Chaucer simply tells his readers how they are to fictionalize themselves" (70). Since there was no established tradition in English for many of the stories, Chaucer uses the frame for what Ong calls "audience readjustment." Although Ong discusses the frame story's didactic purpose, he dismisses it otherwise. "Would it not be helpful," he writes, "to discuss the frame device as a contrivance all but demanded by the literary economy of the time rather than to expatiate on it as a singular stroke of genius? For this it certainly was not, unless we define genius as the ability to make the most of an awkward situation. The frame is really a rather clumsy gambit, although a good narrator can bring it off pretty well when he has to. It hardly has widespread appeal for ordinary readers today" (70).

Except, I would argue, for today's "ordinary readers" who enjoy being *told* a good story in addition to reading one. The fictional storytelling event is still a viable form of presenting an oral tale in literature; there are several contemporary African-American literary works where oral storytelling has been an important component of the text.[16] Contemporary black writers use all three forms of the frame convention: framed, embedded, and frameless. The listener can be inside the text, as in Rita Dove's "The Vibraphone" (1985), or "frameless," as in "The Life You Live (May Not Be Your Own)," by J. California Cooper.[17] This study, then, suggests a way to "read" significant texts in African-American literature–texts which use the spoken-voice storytelling format in some manner–in the context of the frame.

Inside-the-text listeners of African American tales emerged as models for readers in the earliest of African-American fictions. In Frederick Douglass's "The Heroic Slave" (1852), Madison Washington's oral stories moved an initially apolitical Listwell to lean toward abolition. As such, Douglass was using Listwell, as Ong would suggest, as a model for his readers. I contend that African-American fiction writers like Douglass mediate the line between accommodation and resistance to audience demands by opening and sustaining "narrative negotiations" with their audience, negotiations executed through the act of storytelling.

In "'A Little Personal Attention': Storytelling and the Black Audience in Charles W. Chesnutt's *The Conjure Woman*," I suggest that throughout Chesnutt's conjure tales Julius negotiates with John and Annie for increased power and privilege. However, Chesnutt was also negotiating with an African-American readership, however small. As such, the conjure stories can also be seen as an attempt to open the constricting spaces for black individuality in the black community itself. I view the community of enslaved blacks Julius describes in his tale as a microcosm of African America: in part, Chesnutt is negotiating with his implied black frame/audience for increased tolerance of difference among African-Americans *by* African-Americans. Throughout "Hot-Foot Hannibal," then, Chesnutt demonstrates the dual nature of his white and black audiences by subverting the surface-level tale, which seems chiefly concerned with getting two young, white lovers back together, in order to argue for black cooperation.

The second chapter, "'Ah Don't Mean to Bother Wid Tellin' 'Em Nothin': Zora Neale Hurston's Critique of the Storytelling Aesthetic in *Their Eyes Were Watching God*," treats the novel as a long-form storytelling event. To that end, as I discuss Janie's quest to master the storytelling aesthetic–the teller-tale-listener storytelling construct–I disagree with the widespread notion that Janie is telling her tale in order to have Pheoby pass it on to the community. While still a willing participant in the African-American vernacular tradition, the idea that Janie is *consciously* passing the tale on to the community is difficult to sustain. In the process of examining Pheoby as a model for both Eatonville's porch-sitters and the text's readers, it becomes clear by the end of the novel that the *result* of Janie telling her tale is far more problematic than the telling of the tale itself: Janie's exchange with Pheoby in the close frame is contradictory at best. Hurston uses Pheoby as a model for the reader in a slightly different manner than Ong's theory might suggest.

"Listening to the Blues: Ralph Ellison's Trueblood Episode in *Invisible Man*," the third chapter, views the Trueblood episode as crucial to the reading of the novel's depiction of Invisible Man's growth from a naive college student to a mature, knowledgeable individual. Jim Trueblood, who uses the blues to attempt to solve his tragic-comic "ambivalence," emerges as a model (for both Invisible-Man-the-listener and the reader) of what Invisible Man would become in the epilogue: a bluesman. Mr. Norton, who also appears in the epilogue, listens (and *hears*) Trueblood's tale in a different fashion and emerges as a problematic model for readers who identify with him. I also examine the way Ellison, in his epilogue, has his narrator discuss the very nature of audience itself.

James Alan McPherson's "The Story of a Scar," the topic of the fourth chapter, moves the storytelling event to a Northern, urban setting. Aside from expanding the storytelling function from its rural roots, this frame text ably demonstrates that just because a black teller has a black listener doesn't mean that that black teller is a competent listener. The teller in this story must practice audience readjustment with a suspicious *black* listener.

My fifth chapter, "Narrative Negotiations with the Black Aesthetic in Toni Cade Bambara's 'My Man Bovanne,'" demonstrates the way "frameless" frame texts, independent of an explicit frame, negotiate with an *implied* frame. During the late sixties and mid-to-late seventies, some black writers represented spoken-voice storytellers telling first-person tales unencumbered by either a frame or a third-person narrator. By reading the story through Gerald Prince's theory of the Narrator/Narratee, I demonstrate the way Bambara's text works as a fictional argument for artistic autonomy.

John Edgar Wideman's "Doc's Story," like Chesnutt's conjure tales, offers two models for reader identification: a sympathetic black listener and his (ex)girlfriend–a skeptical (potential) white listener. The chief irony rests in the fact that the sympathetic listener, who is also the story's central character, is unsure as to whether the girlfriend "would have believed any of" the tale. As such, "Doc's Story" is an ideal text for a discussion of Stepto's "discourse of distrust" (198), particularly since that distrust is rooted in Wideman's knowledge of and reference to Chesnutt's similar distrust of his readers a hundred years earlier. Wideman's "Doc's Story," then, can be read in several ways: as commentary on the social act of storytelling, as an illustration of a form of "blindness" that connects the interior tale and the external tale, and as direct signification on Chesnutt's dialect tales, thereby bringing this study full circle.

Ultimately, my purpose here is to explore the various written representations of African-American spoken-voice storytelling by African-American writers. Certainly, the existence of stories by writers such as Thomas Nelson Page and Joel Chandler Harris influenced Chesnutt, Paul Laurence Dunbar, and other early writers of black frame texts. I discuss that influence in my Chesnutt chapter, but my focus is on the African-American representation of black spoken-voice storytelling during the century between Chesnutt and Wideman. Without pretending to present a comprehensive account of

African-American frame texts, I will open periodic windows on the black frame text to examine the variety of authorial responses to the convention.

By reexamining the relationship between writer, teller, tale, listener and reader, I will show just how the texts of Chesnutt, Hurston, Ellison, McPherson, Bambara and Wideman alter—sometimes subtly and other times substantially—"traditional" readings of some canonical texts, while establishing readings of non-canonical texts. Altering our angle of vision allows us to shed new light on some "old" texts to produce alternative readings that, while not definitive, do point to the questionable nature of the idea of a "definitive" reading of any text.

From Within the Frame: Storytelling in African-American Fiction, then, probes the tension between the frame and the black spoken voice—and the way that tension manifests itself in different ways, depending on the writer's strategy for accommodating or resisting a particular audience. In the process, this study explores a "spoken" storytelling tradition in African-American literature. By eavesdropping on the conversation between teller and listener inside the text and author and readership outside the text, and then interpreting that conversation, this study professes to tell a critical tale about the role of audience in African-American fiction.

CHAPTER 1

"A little personal attention"
Storytelling and the Black Audience in
Charles W. Chesnutt's *The Conjure Woman*

[T]he Aframerican author faces a special problem which the plain American author knows nothing about—the problem of the double audience. It is more than a double audience; it is a divided audience, an audience made up of two elements with differing and often opposite and antagonistic points of view. His audience is always both white America and black America. The moment a Negro writer takes up his pen or sits down to his typewriter he is immediately called upon to solve, consciously or unconsciously, this problem of the double audience. To whom shall he address himself, to his own black group or to white America? Many a Negro writer has fallen down, as it were, between these two stools.[1]

James Weldon Johnson, quoted here from his 1928 article "The Dilemma of the Negro Author," pinpoints the differing audiences of the African American writer. Double consciousness figures significantly in the way African American writers figure their audience; in a sense, these audience considerations entail Duboisian concepts of both "the color line" and "double consciousness."[2] The question for the black writer, then, is not how to choose between the two audiences—but how to manage them both.

Perhaps Charles Waddell Chesnutt had even more reason than most black writers to fear falling between these "two stools" of audience. For one, he looked, physically, like a white man, and in the 1891 letter to Houghton, Mifflin in which he revealed his race, he ambiguously referred to himself as "an American of acknowledged African descent."[3] He writes, "[T]he infusion of African blood is very small—is not in fact a visible admixture" (69), and then refers to Southern blacks as "they" rather than using the inclusive "we." (Indeed, at one point he uses "these people," two words that have not only historically distanced the user from African Americans, but often infuriated blacks in the process.)

Chesnutt, then, knew just how high the "two stools" of his potential audience were since he was so racially divided genetically, emotionally, and intellectually himself. Johnson, however, comes more to the point: "[I]t is an extremely difficult thing for the Negro author in the United States to address himself solely to either of these two audiences. . . . [O]n one page black America is his whole or main audience, and on the very next page white America" (481). Although he didn't mention him by name in his article, Johnson could very well have been talking specifically about Chesnutt. Chesnutt's fiction, like other black writers before or since, is "framed" by white and black reading audiences, with both audiences having specific needs and demands. It was Chesnutt's task to communicate his ideas and opinions fictionally and yet not "fall . . . as it were, between these two stools."

Although it is doubtful that Chesnutt actually satisfied, to the same extent, both the white and black audiences, it is entirely possible that "Hot-Foot Hannibal," the last story in *The Conjure Woman* (1899), was his best attempt. Chesnutt's text contains a series of interlocking oppositions that revolve around *status* in the plantation community of enslaved Africans. Chesnutt's manipulation of these oppositions—and Hannibal's ultimate subversion of the oppositions—call attention to Chesnutt's message to his African-American readership: the need for a wider space for individual expression within the black community. Although eclipsed somewhat by a shift in narrative focus late in Julius's tale, the message is there nonetheless. Additionally, this critical narrative shift proves to be an example of the difficulty of Chesnutt's attempt to simultaneously accommodate and resist his white readers and yet still, as Johnson puts it, "solve, consciously or unconsciously, this problem of the double audience" (477).

Chesnutt scholars from Robert Bone and Sylvia Lyons Render to William L. Andrews and Richard Brodhead see Chesnutt's use of the frame in *The Conjure Woman* and other dialect stories as his way to address the dual nature of his primarily Northern, white audience.[4] Chesnutt's stories signified on the fiction of Joel Chandler Harris, Thomas Nelson Page and others.[5]

In order to attempt this subversion, Chesnutt needed to "fictionalize" his audience as one which could picture a plantation world far different than the one prevalent in Plantation Tradition stories, but not so different that he couldn't get published at all. Chesnutt's primary consideration was audience and the attempt to change subtly the prevailing ethos of the Plantation Tradition.[6] He offers Uncle Julius McAdoo as the character charged with telling the tale and executing the maneuver. He gives Julius two primary listeners, Northerners John and Annie. John is the amiable-yet-distant, conservative husband of Annie, the sympathetic liberal.

As Lucinda MacKethan points out, Chesnutt's attempt to decenter the Plantation Tradition was not entirely successful. "[R]eaders including the influential William Dean Howells found 'the spells thrown on the simple black lives' Julius depicted to constitute 'enchanting tales.' The public missed completely the ironic inversion[7] by which Julius shows what the white lady listener in the stories can see quite clearly, 'those horrid days before the war.'"[8] Chesnutt attempted to fictionalize his outside-the-text readership by carefully constructing his inside-the-text listening audience–the characters of John and Annie–as skeptical and sympathetic, respectively; he positioned these listeners as the two poles of his intended white audience.

Chesnutt depicted the realities of antebellum slavery far more accurately than did the practitioners of the Plantation School. In Chesnutt's dialect stories, the "peculiar institution" *did* include the selling and separating of children from parents, the threat (and execution) of "fo'ty" lashes upon the backs of enslaved Africans, and a radical exploitation of human labor. By designating John and Annie as a bi-polar audience to set up the all-important, end-of-story readings–and reactions–of those listeners, Chesnutt hoped to influence the white reading public at large in the same way Julius influenced John and Annie.

Chesnutt also attempts, however covertly, to speak to a black readership in *The Conjure Woman*. Not through the frame–there is no black listener in the text–but through the content of Julius's tales. Chesnutt devises an inside-the-text audience as a model for his white readers, but he still has something to say to an African-American audience, no matter how small the readership of the time. Robert Hemenway takes a similar point of view when discussing *Uncle Remus* in his introduction to the 1982 edition. Instead of examining *Uncle Remus* solely as tales told by an elderly black man to a little white boy, Hemenway examines them in their original context: tales told by a black teller to black listeners; or, as the blurb on the back of the book puts it, as they were listened to by "their original American audience–African slaves." Similarly, I see the internal tales Julius tells as existing as a text for black readers of *The Conjure Woman*, with the frame acting as a "mediator, a legitimizer" (Wideman 36) for the larger white audience. The black audience exists as an implied frame around Julius's interior tale.

It is misguided to assume Chesnutt was writing specifically to one white, Northern audience. Critics often cite Chesnutt's journal entry of May 29, 1880:

> I think I must write a book. . . . [I]f I do write, I shall write for a purpose, a high, holy purpose, and this will inspire me to greater effort. The object of my writings would be not so much the elevation of the colored people as the

elevation of the whites,–for I consider the unjust spirit of caste which is so
insidious as to pervade a whole nation, and so powerful as to subject a whole
race and all connected with it to scorn and social ostracism–I consider this a
barrier to the moral progress of the American people; and I would be one of
the first to head a determined, organized crusade against it.[9]

True, this passage does indeed prefigure much of Chesnutt's small canon,
(especially *The Marrow of Tradition* and *The Wife of His Youth and Other Stories
of the Color Line*) and *The Conjure Woman*, which do, indeed, "elevate" whites.
But, in addition, this passage exhibits Chesnutt's concern for the "colored"
people in general and his urge to create an accurate, insider representation of
those folk. Clearly Chesnutt does have a largely white audience in mind as
readers of his fiction. But the above entry is unreliable as the final word on
Chesnutt's audience. Immediately following the above paragraph, he writes,

> This work is of a twofold character. The negro's part is to prepare himself for
> social recognition and equality; and it is the province of literature to open the
> way for him to get it–to accustom the public mind to the idea; and while
> amusing them to lead them on imperceptibly, unconsciously step by step to
> the desired state of feeling. If I can do anything to further this work, and can
> see any likelihood of obtaining success in it, I would gladly devote my life to
> the work. (140)

This last passage can be read two ways. By talking of the "twofold character"
of his "work," Chesnutt could be referring to the way he must formally
"amuse" his readers while "lead[ing] them on." But the "twofold" nature of the
work could also refer to, one, his argument for a literary output that would
instruct the African-American in how to "prepare himself" for social elevation
as well as, two, his urge to construct a body of writing that will then "accustom
the public mind to the idea." If the latter is, as I believe, a viable interpretation,
Chesnutt's double-voiced text carries both aims simultaneously.

But there is another reason Chesnutt's "writ[ing] for . . . the elevation of
whites" comment should not be taken as a total exclusion of a black audience:
Chesnutt was not a man whose opinions and outlook remained static as he
matured. The aforementioned decision to inform Houghton, Mifflin in 1891 of
his African descent, after he allowed Thomas Bailey Aldrich, the editor at the
Atlantic Monthly, to assume otherwise is only one example of his demonstrated
growth. But perhaps the initial journal entry can be most easily judged unreliable by quoting another journal entry, this one dated, not surprisingly, *Friday
the 13th* of August, 1875:

> Well! uneducated people, are the most bigoted, superstitious, hardest headed
> people in the world! Those folks down stairs believe in ghosts, luck, horse
> shoes, cloud signs and all other kinds of nonsense, and all the argument in the
> world couldn't get it out of them. It is useless to argue with such persons. All

the eloquence of a Demosthenes, the logic of Plato, the demonstrations of the most learned men in this world, couldn't convince them of the falsity, the absurdity, the utter impossibility and unreasonableness of such things. . . .

The people don't know words enough for a fellow to carry on a conversation with them. He must reduce his phraseology several degrees lower than that of a first reader, and then all the reason and demonstration has no more effect than a drop of water on a field of dry wheat! "Universal Education" is certainly a much-to-be-wished-for, but, at present, but-little-to-be-hoped-for blessing. (81-82)

This passage certainly appears to contradict the respect for the spirit world in general and conjuring in specific that Chesnutt later displayed in his conjure stories. The passage also demonstrates, if not a contempt for, certainly a frustration with the "folk" that is also surprising, given the seeming sincerity of Uncle Julius's tales. But just as this single passage of a 17-year-old Chesnutt venting his exasperation on a Friday the 13th is revealing, in no way should it be considered the definitive word on his feelings toward black folk. Similarly, his oft-quoted "not so much the elevation of the colored people as the elevation of the whites" sentiments are the equally revealing–but no more definitive–thoughts of a 21-year old. Chesnutt's attitude toward race cannot be glibly inferred by selective references to audience and intent in his journals, particularly since the last journal ends a few months after his twenty-fourth birthday and his publishing did not begin in earnest until five years later, with the publication of "The Goophered Grapevine" in 1887.[10]

Chesnutt's correspondence provides a more reliable portrayal of his audience concerns, since the letters were produced at the time he was actually writing the texts currently under study. For instance, there is evidence that Chesnutt actively sought to place *The Conjure Woman* in black hands, although he was pragmatic about the number of black readers and buyers actually available. He opens a letter to Houghton, Mifflin, dated November 24, 1899, by saying, "During my recent visit to Washington I have been working up more or less interest in my books, and to a certain extent among a class of readers who are not ordinarily large buyers of works of fiction, but who can easily be reached by a little personal attention."[11] He goes on to instruct the publishers to send books to a young black Harvard student, E. French Tyson, to distribute among Washington's middle-class African-American community. In the same letter, he suggests working with a Mr. J. W. Patterson, a "colored man" who, as Chesnutt puts it, "sells [his books] in all sorts of ways–for cash, on time, and on the installment plan, and reaches still another class of readers."[12] Presumably, he means Washington's black working class.

A month later, in December of 1899, Chesnutt wrote a long letter to his publishers providing information about "Afro-American newspapers" and the possibility of advertising his books in them. Chesnutt's letter is typically divided on the topic of race. Of the African-American newspapers, he writes, "Most of them are grossly illiterate, and their readers, generally speaking, buy comparatively few books. . . . Several of the Afro-American newspapers, however, are well-edited, intelligently conducted, and widely read. . . . I was informed by a colored editor . . . that [the following list of newspapers] would reach all the different classes of readers that the colored press appeals to." More importantly, he alludes to just the sort of "insider" status he implied in the first journal entry above when he writes, "I suspect a good many copies of *The Wife of His Youth* will be sold among colored people when they discover, by hearing others speak of it, that it is a book of tracts in their behalf, and written from their side."[13] Indeed, Chesnutt did consider blacks part of his audience, and did address a black audience in *The Conjure Woman*, if only in part. But before I examine the shape of his communication to black readers, a discussion of the controversial publishing history of Chesnutt's stories is in order.

In his introduction to *The Conjure Woman and Other Conjure Tales*, Richard Brodhead outlines the reason it is important to note the order in which Chesnutt's tales were written. The publishing history, Brodhead writes, "supplies a crucial later chapter in the story of Chesnutt's negotiations with a dominant literary order."[14] William L. Andrews considers the publishing history "crucial" as well, and he carefully takes his readers through the order of Chesnutt's early conjure stories. After "The Goophered Grapevine" appeared in 1887, "Po' Sandy" a year later, and then both "The Conjurer's Revenge" and "Dave's Neckliss" in 1889, Chesnutt felt he had taken the frame convention as far as he could. "I think I have about used up the old Negro who serves as mouthpiece," he wrote Albion Tourgée as early as September of 1889, "and I shall drop him in future stories, as well as much of the dialect."[15] Andrews contends that the "'realm of superstition' in which Julius' tales seemed to reside was too narrow to accommodate the writer's increasing seriousness and self-consciousness as an artist. . . . [H]e had decided against entertaining his audience further with the half-fantastic, half-disingenuous dialect reminiscences of Uncle Julius" (22). Andrews sees "Dave's Neckliss" as a transition story away from "romantic conjure" and into "the realm of feeling and passion" (21).

"Dave's Neckliss" was, indeed, written in the midst of Chesnutt's transition period, but that transition went well beyond any single text's thematic concerns. At the end of a two-year span between 1889 and 1891, Chesnutt emerged as a man who was newly, actively engaged in writing essays on the Southern Question and who had begun to explore the varied aspects of the black community, particularly the mulatto condition, as subject matter for his fictions, and as a person of color who was no longer content to let his readers assume he was white. More important than anything else, those two years included critical contact with George Washington Cable. Cable, a man Helen Chesnutt calls "a highly controversial figure in the South" (44n), was, I believe, not quite the cause, but perhaps the catalyst for Chesnutt's developing interest in publicly discussing race. The publication of "The Goophered Grapevine" and "Po' Sandy" in the *Atlantic Monthly* occasioned a congratulatory letter from Cable, who, in February, 1885, "was as famous as any writer in America."[16] Certainly, Chesnutt would find Cable a compelling figure to emulate.[17]

In 1888, Cable was still flush from his success of 1885 and riding the crest of a series of books of fiction and collections of essays. Although Cable's career would eventually be damaged by his strident essay collections on race (*The Silent South* [1885] and *The Negro Question* [1890]), at the specific moment when Chesnutt received Cable's letter congratulating him on publishing his conjure material in the *Atlantic Monthly* in late 1888, Cable must have appeared an excellent example of just the sort of writer Chesnutt hoped to become. Almost all of the personal, careerist and racial considerations that intertwine Cable and Chesnutt are exhibited in this telling excerpt of a letter Chesnutt sent to Cable in early 1889:

> It seems to me that there is a growing demand for literature dealing with the Negro, and for information concerning subjects with which he is in any manner connected—his progress in various parts of the world—in the United States, Brazil, in South America, and in other lands. It seems to me that these subjects would open up a vast field for literary work, and one in which a writer who was connected with these people by ties of blood and still stronger ties of sympathy, could be *facile princeps,* other things being equal, or in which such a writer could at least earn a livelihood. (H. Chesnutt 45)

The implication, based on a reading of Cable's career at this moment, is that the repetition of Chesnutt's phrase "it seems to me" could very possibly mean, "it seems to me, *based on the success* you're *having,*" that "a writer who was connected with these people by ties of blood and still stronger ties of sympathy" could earn a living. This passage echoes the "why could not a colored man" journal entry of March 16, 1880, except here the model is Cable instead of Albion Tourgée.

Chesnutt's "personal acquaintance and friendship"[18] with Cable may have had a far greater impact than heretofore realized. It is after his correspondence with Cable began that his first essay, "An Inside View of the Negro Question," was written. Soon thereafter, "What Is a White Man?" was published in the *Independent* on May 30, 1889. In October, "Dave's Neckliss" appeared in the *Atlantic Monthly.* Less than a year later, on June 5, 1890, Chesnutt wrote to Cable the oft-quoted letter that spoke of his refusal to write about blacks whose "chief virtues have been their dog-like fidelity to their old master, for whom they have been willing to sacrifice almost life itself" (H. Chesnutt 57). Perhaps the culmination of Chesnutt's transition into a racial spokesman is his aforementioned cover letter to the first packet of stories he sent to Houghton, Mifflin in the summer of 1891 in which he openly revealed his race.

Chesnutt's first three Uncle Julius stories were written before the period between 1889 and 1891 when Chesnutt "became deeply interested in this plan to arouse the thinking people of the country in matters so vital to himself and his race" (H. Chesnutt 44). During this transition period he moved beyond the more generalized ambition earlier expressed in his journal of writing for "a high, holy purpose," whereupon "[t]he object of my writings would be not so much the elevation of the colored people as the elevation of the whites" (*Journals* 139). As Sylvia Lyons Render argues, "Though Chesnutt's accurate mirroring of human nature invests his stories with universality, some of them seem specially directed to whites while others have a particular message for blacks"[19]:

> "A Matter of Principle" and "The Wife of His Youth" emphasize through contrast the corrosive effects of color and class prejudice among blacks. "The Partners" is clearly a bid for a pooling of racial talent for joint enterprise; "Tobe's Tribulations" and "Uncle Wellington's Wives" show that blacks must have industry and some kind of salable skill if they wish to avoid following Tobe and Uncle Wellington down to the dead end of failure. "The March of Progress" strongly suggests that blacks should not mistreat persons who have served them well in the past when they are no longer needed. (32)[20]

All of the above stories were written after 1891. And the growth Chesnutt demonstrated during and after his Cable-inspired transition period is reflected in at least three (including "Tobe's Tribulations") of those six additional stories intended to be a part of *The Conjure Woman*. "Mars Jeem's Nightmare,"[21] for example, contains a character that may be modeled after Bras-Coupé, the proud, enslaved African king from Cable's own *The Grandissimes*. "De noo nigger," as Uncle Julius calls the otherwise unnamed character in "Nightmare," is also mysterious, proud, and unwilling and unable to work with the other field slaves. The narrative, for reasons of both plot and societal conformity, eventually reveals the "noo" slave to be a black version of a conjured Mars Jeems–thereby officially "explaining" the presence of this arrogant and imperial enslaved black man. But for the first two-thirds of the story, Chesnutt pushes hard against Plantation Tradition convention as readers are confronted with a fictional representation of the archetypal "bad nigger" who cannot be controlled by typical white force. Curiously, perhaps the best validation of Chesnutt's having undergone a racial transition period between *The Conjure*

Woman's three early stories and the rest of the book is the last story in the collection, "Hot-Foot Hannibal."

I use the word "curiously" only because "Hot-Foot Hannibal" is the one *Conjure Woman* story most often derided as an example of Chesnutt's collapsible accommodation to the demands of his white readers. And there are many examples of that derision: To SallyAnn Ferguson, Uncle Julius is "a mere go-between in a love affair that occupies center stage"[22]; Richard Baldwin writes, "'Hot-Foot Hannibal' comes closer than any other conjure tale to the special group pleading of the propagandist"[23]; Arlene Elder finds the story "the most stereotypic tale in the collection," calling it "the evanescent sweetness of spun-sugar fantasy, not the pungent, bitter root of racial reality"[24]; and Andrews writes, "In the frame of this tale, Julius shows himself a sentimentalist at heart, and he puts his trickery to a traditional end in plantation fiction, the reuniting of white lovers. . . . Julius' machinations and behavior do not upset the frame of the conventional plantation story, which posits the black man's subordination to a white patron's largess. . ." (392). According to Robert Bone "all but one of the seven stories that comprise *The Conjure Woman* are achievements of the first rank"[25]–"Hot Foot Hannibal" turns out to be the lone exception. And in "Aunts, Uncles, Audience: Gender and Genre in Charles Chesnutt's *The Conjure Woman*," Eric Selinger insists that "after enabling the reconciliation of North and South . . . [Julius] softly and silently vanishes."[26]

All of these less-than-flattering comments address the outside frame of the story. Conversely, the internal tale that Julius tells in "Hot-Foot Hannibal" speaks to blacks in ways that no other story in the collection does. Although the inner tale in "Mars Jeems' Nightmare" works well as an explicit black power fantasy, and while the story Julius tells in "Sis' Becky's Pickaninny" is a winning tale of black resistance that includes one of the few unambiguously happy endings in Chesnutt's dialect stories, no other inner tale discusses such intracommunity black concerns as color prejudice and classism. As such, "Hot-Foot Hannibal" emerges as the best story to single out for examination, since the contrast between the outer frame and the inner tale is so great that it is surprising they exist in the same text.[27]

"Hot-Foot Hannibal"'s outer frame story consists of the romantic struggles of Malcolm and Mabel, a young Southern white couple, who resemble the two young lovers in Thomas Nelson Page's "Marse Chan." And Julius, like Sam in "Marse Chan," appears at first glance to be doing all he can to get them back together. According to John's comments in the close frame, Julius told the story so that he could have the option of going to work at the newlyweds' household, assuming their gratitude for the role Julius played toward their being reunited would translate into the offer of a new position.

On the surface, Julius is exerting his agency through the act of storytelling and then negotiating for influence by using storytelling as currency, just as he does in the other stories. This time, however, the negotiation appears not for his benefit but for these two young white lovers. Chesnutt himself, in an essay published the year before his death, spoke to Julius's agency when he said, "In every instance Julius had an axe to grind, for himself or his church, or some member of his family, or a white friend. The introductions to the stories, which were written in the best English I could command, developed the characters of Julius's employers and his own, and the wind-up of each story reveals the old man's ulterior purpose, which, as a general thing, is accomplished."[28]

Writing at the time, in a letter to Walter Hines Page, Chesnutt suggested placing "Hot-Foot Hannibal" last because the story "winds them up well and leaves a good taste in the mouth" (H. Chesnutt 101). The agency Julius demonstrated in the other stories was not at all diminished by his use of storytelling here as a way to "negotiate" for a "white friend." But, as the above quotations indicate, many critics disagree strenuously. Specifically because Julius exerted agency for the benefit of the two young white lovers (and, in part, because it is the last story in the collection), "Hot-Foot Hannibal" has been singled out as an example of the way Chesnutt ultimately portrays Julius as a safe old Uncle, dangerously close to an Uncle Tom.

But the interior tale tells a different story. Chesnutt carefully subverts the external frame story line by having the inner tale transcend the inside-the-text white frame to speak to the outside-the-text black reader. This transcendence is signaled by the tenuous link the inner tale makes to the frame. In most of the other stories, the inner and outer stories are comparable on the thematic level. For example, Julius tells the tale of "Mars Jeems's Nightmare," whose moral is that the better a master treats his enslaved people the more productive they will be, hoping that John will learn the lesson and give Julius's grandson another chance at employment. Similarly, in "The Conjurer's Revenge" there is a direct correlation between the mule John wants to buy and Brer Primus being turned into–and not quite completely turned back from–a mule. Chesnutt, in the cover letter to the packet sent to Houghton, Mifflin containing the six additional conjure stories, asserts that "the outside and inside stories [of "Hot-Foot Hannibal"] are both strong" (H. Chesnutt 94). Actually, I believe he is attesting to the fact that, unlike most of the other stories, there is very little connection between the frame and the inner tale. Only through the use of a late narrative shift, one I will discuss in detail later, does the frame relate to the inner tale.

In that frame, Julius's tale appears designed to tell Mabel, Malcolm Murchison's intended, that loving young couples shouldn't let a small disagreement keep them apart, that they only have so much time together. And

Mabel's response to Julius's story does trigger a reconciliation with her fiance, further solidifying the fact that the interior tale, in service to the frame, was ultimately an effective one. But the story Chesnutt actually has Uncle Julius tell is just one of countless different tales that could have illustrated the temporal nature of loving relationships. Consequently, Julius's tale must be seen as Chesnutt's conscious choice to fill the space inside the frame with the politically charged tale that results.

The story's setting is, of course, the plantation. Frederick Douglass, in *My Bondage and My Freedom*, describes the plantation as "a little nation of its own, having its own language, its own rules, regulations, and customs."[29] Similarly, Charles Scruggs, in *Sweet Home: Invisible Cities in the Afro-American Novel*, talks about a metaphorical place he calls "the invisible city."[30] Although both "nation" and "city," as discreet terms, are inadequate to describe the complex interlocking social relationships among and between enslaved Africans and white slave owners on a large, real-life plantation, the world Chesnutt constructs in Julius's internal tale quickly takes on the characteristics of just such an invisible city. And as Scruggs puts it, "In contemporary black American literature, the invisible city can be anywhere. . . . No matter where the invisible city exists in modern black literature, it must be entered by the 'intimate gate' that Pheoby passes through on her way to Janie's back porch" in *Their Eyes Were Watching God* (216).

As Scruggs emphasizes, "the gate can only be seen by those who know the city by its invisible signs" . . . (216). This is the very metaphorical gate through which Julius passes time and again in the dialect stories. In "Hot-Foot Hannibal," like many of the other stories, Julius suddenly trips the lock to the "intimate gate" of memory by seeing Chloe's "ha'nt"; in other stories the key to the "intimate gate" has ranged from a loudly whirring buzzsaw at a sawmill ("Po' Sandy") and a frog "callin'" in a pond ("Tobe's Tribulations") to the vision of a delicious ham ("Dave's Neckliss"). After seeing or hearing (or tasting) these cues, Julius goes through the gate of memory. In "Hannibal," Julius returns to the "invisible city" of the McAdoo plantation in order to relate the story of Chloe, Jeff, and Hannibal.

While John and Annie[31] cannot accompany Julius through this gate, they watch him as he goes through. In "The Goophered Grapevine," John describes Julius as he begins to tell the tale: "At first the current of his memory–or imagination–seemed somewhat sluggish; but as his embarrassment wore off, his language flowed more freely, and the story acquired perspective and coherence. As he became more and more absorbed in the narrative, his eyes assumed a dreamy expression, and he seemed to lose sight of his auditors, and to be living over again in monologue his life on the old plantation."[32] Likewise, in "Hot-Foot

Hannibal," Julius "began in a subdued tone" (204), suggesting he was again entering the "intimate gate."

Julius's "gate" is, more than anything else, a cultural opening. After he "reads" the plantation as a cultural text for its specific signs–conjuring, escape, constant night travel, a distinct life in the "quarters" that the master cannot penetrate, subtle resistance to excessive exploitation, etc–he hangs those signs onto a plot and thereby translates those signs into a narrative he then, in turn, transmits to John and Annie, his audience. Since they are white and Northern, John and Annie cannot see this "intimate city," and they rely on Julius for his interpretation of life on their land and in their region.

In the tale Julius tells, the lives of Hannibal, Chloe, and Jeff connect and intersect in ways that display the class structure of the McAdoo plantation's African slave community. And to underscore Chesnutt's attempt to speak to a black audience, I stress again that this critique of class and skin color has absolutely nothing to do with the outer tale. Briefly, the story opens with a disagreement between Mabel and Malcolm. Julius appears to manipulate events so that he can tell John, Annie and Mabel (who is Annie's sister) the tale of "Hot-Foot" Hannibal. After telling the tale, Julius drives the coach near the neighboring farm to reunite the two lovers. Inside the frame, however, as in "The Wife of His Youth," Chesnutt wrote a story that spoke to the complex class divisions between blacks–on and off the plantation.

Julius opens his tale by introducing Chloe as "a lackly gal en a smart gal" who works at "de big house" (204). Next, Julius introduces Jeff and Hannibal as two field hands who are called up from the "quarters" by Mars' Dugal' and his wife in order to see which of the two would work at the house and which was to remain in the field. Although initially Hannibal is selected and performs well at his new position, Chloe prefers Jeff and has Aunt Peggy work roots on Hannibal in order to have him replaced with Jeff. After Chloe and Jeff place a "baby doll" under the house, Hannibal begins to feel "light-headed en hot-footed" and makes so many mistakes that he is sent back to the field. His comparison of the two positions is telling:

> Heah th'ee er fo' weeks befo' he'd had a' easy job, waitin' on de w'ite folks, libbin' off'n de fat er de lan', en promus' de fines' gal on de plantation fer a wife in de spring, en now heah he wuz back in de co'n-fiel', wid de oberseah a-cussin' en a-r'arin' ef he did n' get a ha'd tas' done; wid nuffin but co'n bread en bacon en merlasses ter eat; en all de fiel'-han's makin' rema'ks, en pokin' fun at 'im 'ca'se he'e be'n sont back fum de big house ter de fiel'. (213)

There are signal oppositions in the text that determine the tale's conflict. The overriding opposition has to do with status. The "house" slaves have it; the "field" slaves do not. Chesnutt's text reveals this status/non-status opposition by generally portraying lighter skinned blacks as working in the house and darker blacks in the field. These opposites are constructed in such a way that through his manipulation of these signs Chesnutt argues for cooperation not only among the various feuding factions of enslaved Africans on the plantation's "invisible city" but in the late-19th century African-American community as well.

As the above excerpt suggests, house/field represents an important opposition among the enslaved Africans' relations among themselves, because it largely determines the enslaved worker's status both to whites and among the slave population. Those who work in and around the house are seen as possessing a higher social status than, as Hannibal later puts it, "a common, low-down fiel'-han'" (214). As early as the first paragraph of Julius's tale, Chloe, "de fines' gal on de plantation," is described as possessing beauty as well as power and influence at the "big house" as well. She not only has become "mis's own maid," but, according to Julius, "she run de house herse'f, ter heah her talk erbout it" (204). Initially, Chloe doesn't appear at all class conscious. After all, it's not as if she immediately gravitated toward Hannibal simply because the slaveowners chose him over Jeff to work in the big house. When Julius says, "she lack' Jeff, en wuz gwine ter set her sto' by 'im, whuther Mars' Dugal' tuk 'im in de big house er no" (205), it initially appears as if she isn't going to allow the class differences to come between a potential relationship with Jeff. Before long, however, Chloe reveals her class bias when she plans to get Jeff up to the house "in [Hannibal's] place" (205). "Place" is a well-chosen word, because in order to become an appropriate twosome, it appears Jeff's "place" must equal Chloe's: in the house.

Along with the house/field opposition, "Hot-Foot Hannibal" recognizes a light skin/dark skin opposition within the text. Of the three main characters in the tale—Chloe, Jeff, and Hannibal—only Jeff is explicitly referred to by skin color, but other descriptive factors can be used to determine the skin color of Chloe and Hannibal. For example, when Hannibal is demoted and sent back to the field, Julius has Mars' Dugal' say, "'[Y]ou kin sen' dat yaller nigger Jeff up ter de house'" (211). Dugal's use of "yaller" distinguishes Jeff from Hannibal in a way that would be impossible if they were both lightskinned. Similarly, after Hannibal has had his revenge, he tells Chloe, "I got eben wid dat yaller nigger Jeff fer cuttin' me out" (221). And in an earlier paragraph, Hannibal is twice referred to as "dat nigger Hannibal" (205), thereby producing two moments when he could have been referred to as "dat [*yaller*] nigger Hannibal" but was not. Although Hannibal is never explicitly referred to as being dark-skinned, it is likely that he is.

Just as it is likely Hannibal is dark-skinned, it is equally likely that Chloe is *light*-skinned. Julius appears to speak to her skin tone when he says she has "tu'nt pale" (220) and when he describes her as looking "ez pale ez a ghos'" (222). Moreover, when the nineteenth century's prevailing standard of beauty is considered, a woman considered "de fines' gal on de plantation" (213) would almost have to be quite light-skinned indeed.[33] The light/dark, house/field oppositions are sealed to the overall status vs. non-status opposition when Chloe responds to Hannibal's inquiry as to how she and Jeff were "gittin' 'long": "I doan see w'at 'casion any common fiel'-han' has got ter mix in wid de 'fairs er folks w'at lib in de big house" (214). Hannibal's sneering rejoinder confirms the distance between "big house" and "fiel'" when he replies, "No, no! . . . I would n' 'spec' ter be 'vited ter de weddin',–a common, low-down fiel'-han' lack *I* is" (214).

In addition, the enslaved community's reaction to Hannibal's misfortune at the hands of Jeff and Chloe ("all de fiel'-han's makin' rema'ks, en pokin' fun at 'im 'ca'se he'e be'n sont back fum de big house ter de fiel'") speaks directly to the public costs of the loss of status. Certainly, the conflation of light skin with status could not be circumvented by Hannibal or anyone else. But since Hannibal had once had status and lost it, he knew it could be achieved again if he undermined the connection between light skin and house position by exerting his agency in a signal power move.

Before Hannibal's ultimate power play, however, two types of power are exhibited in the tale, thereby forming another opposition: black power vs. white power. In this story, Chesnutt has constituted an "invisible city" where there is the possibility, however slight, of movement from field to house (and, yes, from house back to field), but the determination as to who goes where is, of course, largely in white hands. The world created on the McAdoo plantation in "Hot-Foot Hannibal," regardless of the internecine power struggles among enslaved personnel, is controlled by the white slaveowners. I use the phrase "*largely* in white hands" because the enslaved Africans' alternative to white power in this story, as well as in most of the other tales, is the local conjure woman.

To combat white slaveowner power, Chloe moves toward a power source that is decidedly *off* the plantation–Aunt Peggy. And if Chloe had removed the baby doll as instructed, that power move might have been successful. Interestingly, Chloe's elevated financial status, one that comes from her position in the big house, allows her to buy Aunt Peggy's services: she gives Jeff a silver dollar to give to Aunt Peggy since Jeff had nothing to give.

But when Hannibal dupes Chloe into thinking Jeff has been unfaithful, she doesn't go to Aunt Peggy, as do most characters who've been wronged in the other conjure tales; she heads directly and decisively for the master and tells all, knowing full well that Mars' Dugal' would indeed get "monst'us mad" (218). It is here that the power Aunt Peggy possesses–among blacks *and* whites–is fully revealed:

Mars' Dugal' had warned de han's befo' 'bout foolin' wid conju'ation; fac', he had los' one er two niggers hisse'f fum dey bein' goophered, en he would 'a' had ole Aun' Peggy whip' long ago, *on'y Aun' Peggy wuz a free 'oman, en he wuz 'feard she'd cunjuh him.* En w'iles Mars' Dugal' say he did n' b'liebe in cunj'in en sich, he 'peared ter 'low it wuz bes' ter be on de safe side, en let Aun' Peggy alone. (219 my emphasis)

In the world of *The Conjure Woman*, Dugal' has good reason to be wary of the title character. In "Mars' Jeems' Nightmare," Peggy works her roots on a white slaveowner: "I has ter be kinder keerful 'bout cunj'in w'ite folks" (77), she says in that story–but she goes ahead. And even when Aunt Peggy works on behalf of a white slaveowner, as she does in "The Goophered Grapevine," his employment of her (even at an exploitatively low price) is an implicit acknowledgment of her power to transgress racial boundaries and conjure at will.

But in this story, unlike other conjure stories in which the injured party goes to a conjure man or woman for retribution, Hannibal's revenge on Chloe and Jeff for the baby doll placement comes solely from his own devices. He sets up the false rendezvous, cross-dresses in order to impersonate Chloe,[34] and then watches as Chloe acts in exactly the fashion he anticipates. Hannibal's act of revenge causes Jeff's death and in the process causes Chloe to die of a broken heart. This pivotal power move speaks not only to Chesnutt's usage of non-conjure themes in the ten years since he had stopped writing conjure stories,[35] but also to the non-conjure plotline of "Dave's Neckliss" and his wish to leave conjure behind. Indeed, when viewed solely within the context of his own actions, Hannibal emerges as a remarkably complex character. He is dark and cunning throughout the tale, yet he executes his "big house" duties flawlessly and effortlessly; he does suffer the prolonged effects of Aunt Peggy's baby doll, yet he regains his senses and, totally of his own accord, exacts his revenge. It is doubtful that this highly autonomous character would exist if Chesnutt had written all of the dialect stories at the same time he wrote "The Goophered Grapevine," "Po' Sandy," and "The Conjurer's Revenge."

Moreover, when Hannibal executes his revenge, all of the oppositions come to a head. Here, Hannibal describes his act in his own words in a roadside conversation with Chloe, who has just asked Hannibal what he is "laffin' at":

"'Yah, yah, yah! W'at I laffin' at? W'y I's laffin' at myse'f, tooby sho',–laffin' ter think w'at a fine 'oman I made'. . . . I got squared up wid you fer treatin' me de way you done, en I got eben wid dat yaller nigger Jeff fer cuttin' me out. . . . I sont wo'd ter Jeff dat Sunday dat you wuz gwine ter be ober ter Mars' Marrabo's visitin' dat ebenin', en you want 'im ter meet you down by de crick on de way home en go de rest er de road wid you. En den I put on a frock

en a sunbonnet, en fix' myse'f up ter look lack a 'oman; en w'en Jeff seed me
comin', he run ter meet me, en you seed 'im,–fer I'd be'n watchin' in de
bushes befo' en skivered you comin' down de road. En now I reckon you en
Jeff bofe knows w'at it means to mess wid a nigger lack me.' . . .

"Hannibal had n' mo' d'n finish' w'at he had ter say, w'en Chloe's knees gun
'way unner her, en she fell down in de road, en lay dere half a' hour er so befo'
she come to. W'en she did, she crep' up ter de house des ez pale ez a ghos.'"
(220-22)

When Chloe is displaced as the nominal central character of the tale and
Hannibal is viewed as the tale's chief figure (he is, after all, the title character)
this act of revenge becomes less a villainous act designed to endanger Jeff and
Chloe and more an act of power that allows Hannibal to defeat the various
oppositions which oppress him. Although Hannibal did not resume his "place"
in the house (there is a reference to a "noo house boy" [223] late in the tale),
Hannibal's act itself effectively subverts the status/non-status oppositions.

Further, by having Hannibal execute the act without use of any outside
power source, Chesnutt comments on Chloe's dangerous misuse of McDugal's
white slaveowner power. This tactic eventually spirals out of control when,
finally, she has no authority beyond her initial telling and McDugal's reaction
far surpasses what she would have preferred. Chloe can more easily control
Aunt Peggy's black power than McDugal's white power; even though the
baby doll ruse also grows beyond Chloe's control, it was due to her own error.

Hannibal's independent act speaks to Chesnutt's literary and racial growth
during the time between the writing of the three early stories and those he
wrote later to complete the collection of conjure tales. By having Hannibal
imagine, devise, and execute his plan without access to either white slave-
holder power or black conjure power, Chesnutt, more than anything else,
speaks to the need for individuals to have the opportunity to carve out an
independent space in black culture; if Hannibal can subvert the status opposition while enslaved, Chesnutt seems to be saying, then why can't African-
Americans do it post-bellum?

There is, however, one drawback to Hannibal's victory, one reason why it
can't be called an "ultimate" victory: he's still enslaved.[36] The fact is, he can
only subvert the white/black power opposition to a limited extent while he
remains on the plantation. While white power is the ultimate power on the
"invisible city" of the plantation, in "Hot-Foot Hannibal" Chesnutt moves
beyond the other conjure tales by demonstrating that the usual opposition to
white power, Aunt Peggy's black/conjure power, is not the *only* opposition.

Chesnutt's offering of the triumvirate of Hannibal, Chloe, and Jeff can be
read as a cautionary tale to Negro readers of the time in matters of community. Certainly, this reading is problematized by Chesnutt's own intraracial

prejudices.[37] But when all of the cultural factors are compiled–skin color and class oppositions and their existence beneath white power–and the community voice is considered, it appears Chesnutt's message to the implied black audience is a plea for intraracial cooperation. Chesnutt, in his inner tale that could have been any tale, argues for a world equating the "invisible city" of the McAdoo plantation with the expanded, late-nineteenth century African-American community at large, a community of Blue Vein city dwellers and rural, back-roads sharecroppers united by a racial and cultural bond, to allow a space for all to live with each other comfortably and in harmony. The sum total of all the oppositions seems to be an argument *against* oppositions that have no space in between for someone like Chesnutt himself–a man whose upper middle-class sensibilities are sketchily represented by Chloe but who has an emotional urge to include rather than exclude the Hannibals of the community as well.

It is here, however, as Julius nears the close of his tale, that Chesnutt's message is nearly eclipsed by a critically important narrative disturbance that occurs shortly after the end of the same lengthy passage provided above, when Hannibal disappears from the text. His last words, "'En now I reckon you en Jeff bofe knows w'at it means to mess wid a nigger lack me,'" signal an impending narrative shift: the textual emphasis then sharply veers from the chief, central conflict of Julius's tale–the struggle between Hannibal and Chloe, on behalf of Jeff–to the star-crossed lovers angle. Now that Chloe realizes Jeff and the revealed-to-be sincere love he had for her are both gone, the inner-tale characters Jeff-and-Chloe suddenly resemble outer-tale characters Mable-and-Malcolm. The shift is so abrupt that Hannibal's character instantly ceases to exist; Julius's only additional mention of Hannibal comes at the end of the above passage, in reference to what happened to Chloe when Hannibal finished speaking: "Hannibal had n' mo' d'n finish' w'at he had ter say, w'en Chloe's knees gun 'way unner her, en she fell down in de road, en lay dere half a' hour er so befo' she come to. W'en she did, she crep' up ter de house des ez pale ez a ghos'" (222). Indeed, when Chloe "crep'" away from the scene of her final confrontation with Hannibal, the principal narrative focus creeps away with her.

By necessity, Chesnutt de-emphasizes Hannibal's agency. Far from the foolish lackey the McAdoo enslaved community considers him midway through the tale, Hannibal finally emerges as a trickster figure who knows what he wants and gets it by independent means. And *that* means he must, like the proud and defiant "noo nigger" in "Mars Jeems's Nightmare," disappear. This is the first of two reasons why the tale-ending narrative shift is so important. Hannibal, who exerts his revenge without going to any sanctioned power source, and then *gets away with it*, was a character with far too much autonomous agency for Chesnutt to get into print without a narrative sleight-of-hand. If the outer frame's plot line had made Hannibal the obvious center of the inner tale's narrative, the realities of the literary marketplace would have demanded he have some sort of comeuppance. Here, however, the narrative shift in "Hot-Foot Hannibal" allows white readers to view his actions as simply villainous, and his revenge act can go unpunished because the readers' attention is elsewhere—on the lovers. More importantly, the shift allows the autonomous black male who shuns conjure solutions to walk away unscathed.

The narrative shift is also important formally. Since the short story itself is drawing to a close, the inner tale must be quickly aligned with the outer tale, in which the two estranged lovers—one of which makes up Julius's listening audience—must be reunited. The abruptness of the shift, however, speaks to the difficulty of communicating a dual message to two opposing audiences and amplifies the fact that the two story lines, one for the outer frame and the other for the inner tale, are essentially incompatible.

In "Hot-Foot Hannibal," the frame exists in direct opposition to the black-themed interior tale. As mentioned above, in the other dialect stories Julius tells tales that subvert the plantation tradition, either by exhibiting the transient nature of the "monst'us good" worker or merely by talking frankly and matter-of-factly about the brutality and harshness of slavery. Most of the conjure stories have frames that don't refer explicitly to slavery at all, with occasional exceptions such as the close frame of "Po' Sandy," where Annie says, "What a system it was . . . under which such things were possible!" (60), or John's comment in the open frame of "The Gray Wolf's Ha'nt,": "But even the wildest [of Julius's tales] was not without an element of pathos,—the tragedy, it might be of the story itself; the shadow, never absent, of slavery and of ignorance; the sadness, always, of life as seen by the fading light of an old man's memory" (168). Julius's interior tales do subvert the plantation tradition. But on the whole they seem to confirm Chesnutt's "elevation of whites" comment from his *Journal*: his primary function is to overturn white racist attitudes with his fictions.

"Hot-Foot Hannibal," however, is the best example of Chesnutt's difficulty in using the outer frame to accommodate the prevailing race-specific dictates of the plantation tradition while simultaneously using the inner tale to speak to a black audience. The narrative shift that occurs with the end of Hannibal's revenge act is the critical point where resistance collapses and accommodation returns. By adapting the convention of the plantation tradition, yet communicating a covert, subterranean message to black audiences, Chesnutt was simultaneously accommodating and resisting the cultural box out of which he was writing. As Johnson so aptly put it, the American audience "is more than a double audience; it is a divided audience, an audience made up of two elements with differing and often opposite and antagonistic points of view" (477). Audience considerations, both within and without the text, drove the narrative focus to be placed where it was–and for it to be moved when it was. With this reading, "Hot-Foot Hannibal" assumes a new dimension. The story becomes an excellent example of the difficulty of balancing accommodation and resistance to divergent audiences in African-American fiction at a time when such accommodation was expected, and resistance had to be coded and subversive in order to get into print at all.

Although Charles Chesnutt published the majority of his work around the turn of the century, many African-American writers were still struggling in the late thirties with many of the same audience concerns that Chesnutt wrestled with when he published *The Conjure Woman*; indeed, many are still considerations today. Less than ten years after James Weldon Johnson's "The Dilemma of the Negro Author," J. B. Lippencott published what was to become Zora Neale Hurston's most well-known novel, *Their Eyes Were Watching God* (1937).

Like Chesnutt, Hurston was aware of her "double audience."[38] "Structurally," writes Henry Louis Gates, Jr. and Sieglinde Lemke, "most of [Hurston's] narratives are framed tales, with a story within a story, as in *Their Eyes Were Watching God*" (xxii). And frame texts, with one character telling of a story to another, require a relationship with audience. Whether it's explicit or implicit, or whether it has to do with the standard teller-listener relationship, frame stories and frame novels both suggest an audience beyond the common writer/reader relationship. Chesnutt, as we have seen, had yet another, implied audience. Hurston, as I discuss in my next chapter, also has multiple audiences in mind.

CHAPTER 2

"Ah don't mean to bother wid tellin' 'em nothin'"

Zora Neale Hurston's Critique of the Storytelling Aesthetic in *Their Eyes Were Watching God*

While they differ in genre, Zora Neale Hurston's novel is similar in form to Charles Chesnutt's dialect stories. Both have tellers and listeners, and both have open and close frames. As Henry Louis Gates, Jr. writes, "to narrate this tale, Hurston draws upon the framing device, which serves on the order of plot to interrupt the received narrative flow of the linear narration of the realistic novel, and which serves on the order of theme to enable Janie to recapitulate, control, and narrate her own story of becoming, the key sign of sophisticated understanding of the self."[1] The difference between Chesnutt and Hurston is that, as Gates continues, "The text opens and ends in the third-person omniscient voice, which allows for a maximum of information-giving" (185). This also means that Pheoby Watson doesn't need to be the framing narrator/listener. As such, Hurston's portrayal of Pheoby as a viable character who plays a significant role in the tale itself—instead of having her remain a largely external listener/narrator—allows for a more in-depth reading of Pheoby as model. Pheoby models for both the porch-sitters inside the text and the readers outside the text. Her critical position as listener—and even more importantly, *reactor*—to Janie's tale suggests a way for the book's readers to respond to the tale and novel, even though Hurston, as we shall see, complicates that suggestion in the close frame. Phoebe's role as listener/potential teller suggests the way she will relate Janie's story to the porch-dwellers—if she chooses to do so. So Pheoby, in this text, performs triple duty: she is listener/model for the porch-sitters, she is listener/model for the readership, and she is an instrumental character in the tale as well. While Hurston's portrayal of Janie is informed by her ideas about gender roles, patriarchy and community, it is through the interaction of Janie-the-teller and Pheoby-the-listener that Hurston communicates her ideas about storytelling. In *Their Eyes Were Watching God*, Hurston critiques the storytelling aesthetic and Pheoby is the hub, the geometrical "point" through which the teller, the community (as potential listeners), and the readership all must pass on the way to meaning.

Janie talks to Pheoby in the open frame (all of chapter one) and the close frame (roughly the last two pages of the novel). In between is a long interior tale told through Janie to Pheoby in the third-person point of view.[2] The text is circular; the readers, in that open frame, are not only told of Janie's return to Eatonville, but are told, as early as the third paragraph, that she "had come back from burying the dead"[3] and that the people "sitting on porches beside the road" (1) are envious "from other times" (2). Finally, readers are told, frankly, "Tea Cake gone" (7). Just as Ralph Ellison's *Invisible Man* begins at the end and ends at the beginning, Hurston both sets up and concludes much of the tale in the open frame. Later, in Hurston's short close frame, Janie settles in to enjoy the horizon. In between, she sits on her back porch and "tells" Pheoby, through that peculiar third-person point of view, what she experienced while she was away. Much has been written on the orality of the novel,[4] and the fact that Janie Crawford is, as Mary Helen Washington writes in her foreword to the Perennial Library edition, "powerful, articulate, self-reliant, and radically different from any woman character . . . ever before encountered in literature."[5] Gates, moreover, calls Zora Neale Hurston "the first writer that our generation of black and feminist critics has brought into the canon. . . . a cardinal figure" who invites "increasingly close readings, which Hurston's texts sustain delightfully" (180).

There have, indeed, been "increasingly close readings" of *Their Eyes*, and the narrative strategy Hurston employs has constituted a large part of those readings. But a different reading surfaces when *Their Eyes Were Watching God* is viewed as a novel-length storytelling event. First, Hurston chronicles Janie's long quest to master the storytelling aesthetic, a term I discuss in depth below. She then interrogates that aesthetic as she alters the core–the sacred teller-tale-listener construct–by refusing to execute the "traditional" teller-to-community storytelling function. Finally, Hurston critiques her audiences, both inside and outside the text, as she displays, in the close frame, a telling ambivalence towards audience that spreads a layer of complexity over the storytelling aesthetic itself.

There are three interrelated components to storytelling: the teller, the tale, and the listener(s). Once past that certainty, however, storytelling definitions disagree. As Anne Pellowski writes, "There is not only much disagreement about the words 'tell,' 'teller,' and 'telling' and their use to describe both oral and written processes; the term 'story' is also the subject of much discussion."[6]

It is not necessary, for the purposes of this discussion, to concretely "define" storytelling, but a brief discussion of what I mean when I use the term "storytelling aesthetic" *is* necessary, because Janie's attempt to master that aesthetic constitutes the first fourteen chapters of the novel. In short, when a storytelling aficionado demonstrates the ability to perform all three roles of the storytelling act–if he or she can effectively tell a "big" tale, and, at other times, practice attentive and empathetic listening–he or she has mastered the storytelling aesthetic.

Janie approaches this aesthetic through the personal narrative; her tale assembles the details and incidents in her life–and the way she feels about those moments she describes. Linda Dégh, in *Narratives in Society: A Performer-Centered Study of Narration*, calls personal narratives "Histories of life experiences, encountering, creating, and being affected by events [that become] inexhaustible sources of folklore in the modern world."[7] More importantly, writes Dégh, "With personal stories the teller not only claims authorship but also plays the role of participant and eventually that of central hero . . ." (77).

But while Dégh's subtitle reveals her emphasis on the teller, Geneva Smitherman, in *Talkin and Testifyin*, argues that centuries-old African "group norms are balanced by infivualized, improvisational emphases. By virtue of unique contributions to the group-approved communicative structure, the individual can actualize his or her sense of self within the confines of the group."[8] The African-American vernacular process of call and response, writes Smitherman, recalls that "the traditional African world view conceptualizes a cosmos which is an interacting, interdependent, balanced force field. The community of men and women, the organization of society itself, is thus based on this assumption. Consequently, communication takes on an interactive, interdependent nature. . . . [C]all-response seeks to synthesize speakers and listeners in a unified movement" (108). Ultimately, Dégh agrees: "[T]he etiquette of storytelling is a part of cultural learning in traditional rural societies. The folk sets high standards for how tales must be told, developing a code of aesthetics to normalize the use of . . . linguistic and semiotic formulas. . . . Storytellers are judged . . . by their degree of imagination, original story development, structuring, and the bridging of everyday reality with fiction in the formulaic introduction and closure of a story" (9).

This all-encompassing storytelling "aesthetic" refers to the relationship between the teller, the tale, and the audience. As important as the teller is, the listeners are "judging" the storyteller–and his or her tale–and in the process the audience is *collaborating* with the teller on the establishment and maintenance of the storytelling aesthetic. Proficiency in storytelling, then, demands competency in all three aspects of storytelling because, as the preface to *Talk*

That Talk: An Anthology of African-American Storytelling insists, "The storyteller, the story, and the audience are of equal importance."[9]

When Janie and Jody Starks first move to Eatonville, Janie obviously has little knowledge of storytelling as an aesthetic. After Tony Taylor officially moves to make Starks the mayor at the first town meeting, he says, "And now we'll listen tuh uh few words uh encouragement from Mrs. Mayor Starks." But Jody interrupts, saying, "Thank yuh fuh yo' compliments, but mah wife don't know nothin' 'bout no speech-makin'. Ah never married her for nothin' lak dat. She's uh woman and her place is in de home" (40-1). Janie's response is telling: unaware of the give and take of public orality, "[s]he had never thought of making a speech, and didn't know if she cared to make one at all." But she did know that "the way Joe spoke out without giving her a chance to say anything one way or another . . . took the bloom off things" (41). This is the moment, notwithstanding her subdued participation in the telling of Nanny's "text" earlier in the narrative,[10] that she first becomes aware of the teller-tale-listener construct—the storytelling aesthetic—and the difficulty she will have finding a role in the community discourse.

From this point on, Janie struggles first merely to participate in, and then to master, the storytelling aesthetic. Although she doesn't realize it at the time, Janie would attempt to become well-versed in all three aspects of the storytelling aesthetic, and her just-described, initial, unsatisfactory encounter with the porch-sitters reveals just how far she must travel to become the storytelling participant she wants to be. Hurston demonstrates Janie's growing interest in storytelling in the opening of the next chapter: "The store itself was a pleasant place if only she didn't have to sell things. When the people sat around on the porch and passed around the pictures of their thoughts for the others to look at and see, it was nice. The fact that the thought pictures were always crayon enlargements of life made it even nicer to listen to" (48). Janie readily recognizes the pleasures of the storytelling event, and for the most part this sixth chapter is devoted to word "pictures," and the way Jody repeatedly interrupts any of Janie's attempts to participate in telling them.

In "the case of Matt Bonner's yellow mule," for instance, "Janie loved the conversation and sometimes she thought up good stories on the mule, but Joe had forbidden her to indulge. Just when Lige or Sam or Walter or some of the other big picture talkers were using a side of the world for a canvas, Joe would hustle her off inside the store to sell something. Look like he took pleasure in doing it" (50-1). Indeed, much of the difficulty Janie has in her attempts to master the storytelling aesthetic stems from the patriarchal sexism that surrounds the store. Janie's struggle to gain proficiency of the storytelling aesthetic involves grappling with the sexist assumptions of the men of Eatonville. As she works toward the former, she must also triumph over the latter.

Ironically, when Joe buys and "retires" Bonner's mule, Janie surprises the porch-sitters by publicly congratulating him. When she compares him to Abraham Lincoln ("Lincoln he had de whole United States tuh rule so he freed de Negroes. You got uh town so you freed uh mule. You have tuh have power tuh free things and dat makes you lak uh king uh something"), Hambo says to Joe, "Yo' wife is uh born orator, Starks. Us never knowed dat befo'. She put jus' de right words tuh our thoughts" (55). Still, although obviously pleased and flattered, Starks forbids her to express her gift.

Starks, as he makes clear in the above a-woman's-place-is-in-the-home comment, is following a patriarchal model for his leadership of the town. But he also takes a class-based attitude to Janie's activities. Throughout chapter six he repeatedly separates Janie from the cultural folk-life of the townspeople. For instance, everybody indulges in "mule talk" except Janie because Joe "didn't want her talking after such trashy people" (50). Similarly, he is aghast at Janie's wanting to go to the "draggin'-out" of Matt Bonner's mule: "Ah'm uh man even if Ah is de Mayor. But de mayor's wife is somethin' different again . . . *you* ain't goin' off in all dat mess uh commonness. Ah'm surprised at yuh fuh askin'" (56).

Starks prevents Janie from telling any tales, and he also interrupts her listening enjoyment. For instance, when Daisy Blunt comes down the street "walking a drum tune" (63) and all of the single men crowd around her, Dave and Jim get into a contest about who loves her most. The competition builds in humor until "There was one of those big blow-out laughs and Janie was wallowing in it. Then Jody ruined it all for her" (65) by insisting Janie wait on Mrs. Bogle inside the store. Janie obviously feels it's important to be a part of the audience on the porch, and she is disappointed when she has to leave: "Janie wanted to hear the rest of the play-acting and how it ended, but she got up sullenly and went inside. She came back to the porch with her bristles sticking out all over her and with dissatisfaction written all over her face" (66). Janie wants to participate but is blocked by Jody's need for control over her cultural activities.

The chapter ends with Janie doing "what she had never done before, that is, thrust[ing] herself into the conversation" (70). In this case, the text earmarks her entry into porch discourse in an obvious and significant way, and what she actually says is as noteworthy as the interruption itself:

> "Sometimes God gits familiar wid us womenfolks too and talks His inside business. He told me how surprised He was 'bout y'all turning out so smart after Him makin' yuh different; and how surprised y'all is goin' tuh be if you ever find out you don't know half as much 'bout us as you think you do. It's so easy to make yo'self out God Almighty when you ain't got nothin' tuh strain against but women and chickens." (70-71)

This statement becomes a signal that she is beginning to exercise her agency, particularly when contrasted with her previous public comment comparing Starks with kings and U.S. presidents and his "power tuh free things" (55). Here Janie speaks spontaneously and from the heart; her words above are in reaction to a conversation in which Jim Stone, Walter Thomas and Lee Coker endorse wife-beating as they castigate Tony Taylor for treating his wife too nicely (70). Janie is gradually beginning to free herself from Jody's control—if not her body, certainly her tongue.

Indeed, the next chapter begins with the narrator's saying Janie "had learned how to talk some and leave some" (72). And although the narrative jumps eleven years ahead in between chapters, there are only four pages between the above first-time interruption and her oft-quoted comment, "When you pull down yo' britches, you look lak de change uh life" (75). The strident public voice she uses to stop Starks from criticizing her age and body compares to the "big voice" Starks usually has, but when he realizes the town's reaction ("Ah ruther be shot with tacks than tuh hear dat 'bout mahself," Lige Moss says [75]), he is, literally, rendered speechless. As she asserts her will to transcend the gender boundaries Starks has placed upon her, Janie also takes yet another step—a big one—toward mastery of the storytelling aesthetic by publicly expressing her voice.

After Jody's death, Janie becomes an increasingly active, participatory audience member on the store porch. Starks made it difficult for her storytelling prowess to grow while he was alive. But during her marriage to Tea Cake who, unlike Starks, encouraged her to participate in common folk practices instead of thinking she belonged "above" them, Janie became a fully-integrated audience-member-and-teller-of-tales down on the muck. The signal moment of Janie's audience awareness comes late in chapter fourteen when she reflects on how far she's come as a participant in the vernacular tradition.

> Sometimes Janie would think of the old days in the big white house and the store and laugh to herself. What if Eatonville could see her now in her blue denim overalls and heavy shoes? The crowd of people around her and a dice game on her floor! She was sorry for *her friends* back there and scornful of *the others*. The men held big arguments here like they used to do on the store porch. Only here, she could listen and laugh and even talk some herself if she wanted to. *She got so she could tell big stories herself from listening to the rest.* (127-8, italics mine)

Janie is referring to a split audience—"her friends," chief among them Pheoby—versus "the others" on the porch who objected to Janie's relationship with Tea Cake. This passage signals that she has successfully integrated all three aspects—teller, tale, and audience—of the storytelling aesthetic: she was already an excellent audience member, and she can now tell "big stories" herself.

Since she is now competent in all phases of the storytelling event, Janie, in both the open and close frames, sees two distinctly different audiences as possible listeners for her tale. As Gates points out, "the word *voice* recurs with great frequency" in the novel, and he contends that "who sees and who hears at all points in the text remain fundamental as well" (200, italics in text). Her "friends," represented by Pheoby, constitute one potential audience. The porch-sitters, whom Janie derisively refers to as "Mouth-Almighty" (5), represent another.

Having returned from the muck a fully-realized storyteller, Janie has a view of the porch-sitters that contrasts sharply from that of critics such as Missy Dehn Kubitschek, who assert that by "emphasizing the frame story and the pattern of the quest, Hurston extends the narrative pattern to include the effects of the heroine's ascent and immersion on the community." Reading Hurston through Robert Stepto's *From Behind the Veil*, Kubitschek sees Janie as an "articulate kinsman," someone who "influences an initial audience (Pheoby) and has reason to anticipate an expanded audience and extended effects for her art. *Their Eyes Were Watching God*, then, intimates a third narrative, this time a group ascent."[11] This "group ascent" argument, however, does not take into account Janie's stated attitude toward that "expanded audience."

For although they would love to hear it first hand, the people sitting on Pheoby Watson's porch–Pearl Stone, Lulu Moss, Mrs. Sumpkins, among others–are left right where they are as Janie walks on by, heading home from the muck. Janie does not invite them to listen to her tale. But these porch-sitters do take this opportunity to remind the reader–and Pheoby–of the fate of Annie Tyler and Who Flung, and the porch-sitters' early, page-two commentary becomes a sub-narrative that serves as a stubborn cautionary tale throughout the text. The Tyler-Who Flung narrative is at least a minor consideration of almost every major character in the novel at one time or another. The differing reactions of the community of Eatonville to the Tyler-Who Flung narrative is a good way to explore several contrasting and interlocking relationships: Janie to the community at large, Janie to Tea Cake, Janie to Pheoby, and, perhaps most importantly, Janie to the porch-sitters. In a sense, the Tyler-Who Flung narrative acts as a lens through which readers can view the Eatonville community and its social mores. It shows why Janie refused to tell the community her tale and displays a sense of Janie's multiple audiences.

In the open frame, the porch-sitters think they know why Janie has returned: what happened to Annie Tyler must have happened to Janie, too. Sometime before Tea Cake came to town, Tyler, an older woman, proudly and confidently left Eatonville with a younger man named Who Flung, who soon took her money and abandoned her in Tampa. From the porch-sitters' vantage point, perhaps the most important sentence in the novel is this one:

"[Tyler] was broken and her pride was gone, so she told those who asked what had happened" (114). The sentence's construction makes it appear that Tyler tells her tale *because* she is "broken" and has nothing left. The beyond-shame narrative Tyler tells, then, informs the porch-sitters' view of Janie–an older woman they once held up as "Mrs. Mayor Starks" who returns home alone one evening wearing grubby "overhalls" a year-and-a-half after leaving town with a good-looking younger man.[12]

The porch-sitters may be the first to mention the Tyler-Who Flung narrative as an explanation for Janie's return, but even before she leaves to meet Tea Cake, Pheoby insists Janie take two hundred dollars with her, urging her to "keep it secret just to be on the safe side" (112). Later, when Janie returns from the muck, Pheoby reveals what she meant by staying "safe" when she tells Janie, "You better make haste and tell [the porch-sitters] 'bout you and Tea Cake gettin' married, and if he taken all yo' money and went off wid some young gal, and where at he is now and where at is all yo' clothes dat you got to come back here in overhalls" (6). Obviously Pheoby thought Annie Tyler's abandonment would–and had–happened to Janie as well.

Although she dismisses Phoebe's assumption, at one point in her tale *Janie*, in fact, was concerned that the Tyler-Who Flung narrative would become her own. On her first morning in Jacksonville, after she drowsily sends Tea Cake out to find some breakfast fish, Janie falls back to sleep, wakes up to find her money gone, and then doesn't see Tea Cake again for over twenty-four hours. "All day and night she worried time like a bone," writes the narrator, and "[w]ay late in the morning the thought of Annie Tyler and Who Flung came to pay her a visit" (113).

It is here that Hurston gives the details of Annie Tyler's involvement with Who Flung, and immediately some stark differences between Annie Tyler and Janie Crawford arise. As Janie sits alone in her room thinking about Annie Tyler and wondering if Tea Cake will return, the narrator writes that Tyler had, like Janie, "been left a widow with a good home and insurance money" (113). Unlike Janie, however, Tyler soon had "dyed hair, newly straightened," and "uncomfortable new false teeth," and, always, "her giggle." The narrator then describes Tyler's "love affairs," in which she spent her "ready cash" on young men until it was gone. *Then* Who Flung came along to persuade her to sell her house and move to Tampa. Perhaps the most obvious difference between Annie Tyler and Janie is demonstrated by the description of how they each left town:

> Jacksonville. Tea Cake's letter had said Jacksonville. . . . No need for Janie to wait any longer. Wear the new blue dress because he meant to marry her right from the train. . . . Janie's train left too early in the day for the town to witness much, but the few who saw her leave bore plenty witness. They had

to give it to her, she sho looked good, but she had no business to do it. It was hard to love a woman that always made you feel so wishful. (111)

Conversely,

The town had seen [Annie Tyler] limp off. The undersized high-heel slippers were punishing her tired feet that looked like bunions all over. Her body squeezed and crowded into a tight corset that shoved her middle up under her chin. But she had gone off laughing and sure. As sure as Janie had been. (113-14)

And yet, the possibility that Tea Cake might not come back prompts Janie to think briefly about the way Tyler "had waited all her life for something, and it had killed her when it found her" (114). Before long, Janie realizes the chief difference between herself and Tyler: "[Janie] had ten dollars in her pocket and twelve hundred in the bank" (115). But her consideration of the Tyler-Who Flung narrative has an effect on her nevertheless: "God, please suh, don't let him love nobody else but me. Maybe Ah'm is uh fool, Lawd, lak dey say, but Lawd, Ah been so lonesome, and Ah been waitin', Jesus. Ah done waited uh long time" (115). For his part, when Tea Cake returns to find Janie "settin' on de floor" after spending the night with "her head in a rocking chair" (115), he guesses, without any prompting, that she has assumed that the Tyler-Who Flung narrative was about to repeat itself. "Ah see whut it is," he says. "You doubted me 'bout de money. Thought Ah had took it and gone. Ah don't blame yuh but it wasn't lak you think. De girl baby ain't born and her mama is dead, dat can git me tuh spend our money on her" (115-16). Tea Cake tells Janie why he was absent,[13] and Janie and Tea Cake are inseparable from then on.

The porch-sitters' early reaction to Janie walking into town at sundown wearing a "faded shirt and muddy overalls" (2)–especially given her blue satin departure–is not surprising, given the dominance of the Tyler-Who Flung narrative in the imagination of the town:

"What she doin' coming back here in dem overhalls? Can't she find no dress to put on?–Where's dat blue satin dress she left here in?–Where all dat money her husband took and died and left her?–What dat ole forty year ole 'oman doin' wid her hair swingin' down her back lak some young gal?– Where she left dat young lad of a boy she went off here wid?–Thought she was going to marry?–Where he left *her?*–What he done wid all her money?– Betcha he off wid some gal so young she ain't even got no hairs–why she don't stay in her class?–" (2, italics in text)

When the town emphasizes "her" as they ask, "Where he left *her?*" they are implicitly comparing Janie to the memory of Annie Tyler's return. The stubborn existence of the Tyler-Who Flung narrative is a vivid, recent reminder of disastrous May-December relationships, and becomes a narrative Janie must contend with on all fronts, including the one in her own mind. As such, Janie's successful relationship with Tea Cake is a corrective to Tyler's troubles with Who Flung.

Perhaps most importantly, however, the Tyler-Who Flung narrative acts as a litmus test. The reaction to Janie's return—and the degree to which she's compared to Annie Tyler—shows just how much (or little) the townspeople can receive Janie's tale fairly, how much they must change, and how far they must come in order to become "competent" listeners.[14] Phoebe's friendship with Janie, although perhaps not as rock-solid as a surface-level reading of the novel suggests, at least allows her access to the tale Janie tells, and as a result she is able to shed her initial, incorrect assumption about what happened to Janie. But the porch-sitters have such a strong belief in the truth—for them—of what happened to Annie Tyler that Janie denies them direct access to her corrective tale, believing them to be incompetent listeners. The Tyler-Who Flung narrative's presence in the text—and the town's willingness to apply the narrative—is the biggest example of the difficulty Janie would have to make a storytelling connection with the porch-sitters. Janie's mastery of the story-telling aesthetic, confirmed from her experiences in the muck, allows her to view the porch-sitters as an unfavorable audience.

But even Pheoby, as we have seen, incorrectly anticipates Janie's story, just as the porch-sitters do. In fact, Phoebe's dual status as porch-sitter and friend-of-Janie, places her in a peculiar position as listener/model for Hurston's readers.[15] Pheoby does defend Janie as she returns to town from the muck, saying to the other porch-sitters, "[Y]ou mad 'cause she didn't stop and tell us all her business. . . . Y'all makes me tired. De way you talkin' you'd think de folks in dis town didn't do nothin' in de bed 'cept praise de Lawd. You have to 'scuse me, 'cause Ah'm bound to go take her some supper." Then the narrator says she "stood up sharply" (3) as if she was angry. But when she tells Janie a short time later that she only hears what the porch-sitters say because they "collect round [her] porch 'cause it's on de big road," she understates her involvement and identification with the porch-sitters. It is, after all, only a few paragraphs later that she urges Janie to tell them what happened.

Certainly, Phoebe's dual identity as acquaintance to the porch-sitters and friend to Janie is difficult to sustain. John Callahan aptly describes the porch-sitters as people who "use words falsely and meanly, without spirit . . . [people who] fear the vital, realized self of one of their own who has broken their rules and survived to tell the story."[16] But although Pheoby is Janie's friend, she also shares some of the porch-sitters' less appealing characteristics. Pheoby urges Janie to "make haste" and tell the porch-sitters her tale in the open frame, and in chapter twelve she brings the porch-sitter's "concern" about Janie's growing relationship with Tea Cake to Janie's attention: "Janie, *everybody's talkin'* 'bout how dat Tea Cake is draggin' you round tuh places you ain't used tuh." And, *"Folks seen you* out in colors and *dey thinks* you ain't payin' de right amount uh respect tuh yo' dead husband" (107, italics added). Moreover, her concern is prompted by a pillow-talk conversation Pheoby had the night before with Sam Watson, her husband, during which he says, *"De men wuz talkin'* 'bout it in de grove tuhday and givin' her and Tea Cake both de devil" (106 italics added).

Even if the porch-sitters do, as Callahan puts it, "use words falsely and meanly, without spirit," Pheoby certainly appears to be taking them seriously enough. She acts, perhaps unconsciously, as intermediary between Janie and the porch-sitters, and she delivers those "false" and "mean" words to her friend. Her friendship with Janie is, to a certain extent, *balanced* by porch-sitting "concerns." Phoebe's eagerness to hear what happened during Janie's year-and-a-half away from Eatonville also hints at her dual allegiance. The narrator portrays Pheoby as "eager to feel and do through Janie, but hating to show her zest for fear it might be thought mere curiosity" (6). Moments later, she "dilated all over with eagerness" (7). Again, Phoebe's dual identity status troubles these descriptions. In one sense, she's simply eager to hear what happened to her "best friend." In another, as a result of her porch-sitting experience, she appears *wary* of "show[ing] her zest" because it might be mistaken for the sort of "mere curiosity" the porch-sitters would exhibit.

When Pheoby sits down to listen to Janie, she is keenly aware of the possibility of her words or actions being misinterpreted, and it's not the first time. A previous example is the circuitous route she takes to Janie's house to report what the porch-sitters were saying about Janie and Tea Cake:

> The next morning Pheoby picked her way over to Janie's house like a hen to a neighbor's garden. Stopped and talked a little to everyone she met, turned aside momentarily to pause at a porch or two–going straight by walking crooked. So her firm intention looked like an accident and she didn't have to give her opinion to folks along the way. (107)

Just as she feels a need to hide her eagerness to hear Janie's story, in the passage above she hides her intention to speak with Janie by "going straight by walking crooked." Both scenarios require an acute awareness of the gaze of onlookers, predicting their reaction, and then acting accordingly. Her association with the porch-sitters has inflated her sense of their importance and has taught her to cloak her intentions. But it is this same porch-sitter-influenced behavior that informs her own actions, as we have seen above, with Janie. Since Janie does give Pheoby permission to tell the porch-sitters her story, Pheoby is absolved of the difficulty of possessing Janie's story without permission to repeat it. But the dual identity Pheoby possesses complicates the way readers interpret her actions.

Pheoby, as sole listener to Janie's tale and model for Hurston's readership, has a complicated role to play. She is a close confidant of the teller, yet she also has a steady relationship with the people on the porch. This disquieting dual status explains the ambiguous statement Pheoby makes to Mrs. Sumpkins just before she leaves to greet Janie on her arrival home: "If she got anything to tell yuh, you'll hear it" (4). Callahan contends that with this comment Pheoby "creats a nest" for Janie's story, that she "asserts Janie's right to choose her space and her audience" (122). However, Phoebe's dual identity gives her parting comment to Mrs. Sumpkins more than one meaning. The sentence changes based on how one views Phoebe's relationship with the porch-sitters. If, as Callahan contends, Pheoby is seen as protector of Janie's story, it means, *If she allows me to tell you anything, I will.* If Pheoby is, as I contend, a woman who struggles with her dual identity, the sentence could mean, *If I determine she's got anything for you to hear, I'll tell you.* The former relies foursquare on Janie's agency. The latter relies on Phoebe's. Ultimately, Janie, who is, as Callahan writes,

> sufficiently a friend to her own story and its telling to resist the prurient interest of Eatonville, understands and accepts Phoebe's position. She is unthreatened by Phoebe's double identity as a friend to her and a fully accepted member of the community. True to intimacy, Janie does not ask for total allegiance from Pheoby; in her proud, confident autonomy, she seeks only that fair, open, honest hearing appropriate to friendship and storytelling. Rather than set ground rules, Janie allows Pheoby the freedom to retell what she will hear. (123)

And if she does retell the story, this intimate exchange *can*, then, benefit Eatonville's community. But Janie's original motive was, as Callahan implies, far more modest.

In fact, it is here, in the open and close frame, where Janie's hard-won acquisition of the storytelling aesthetic comes into play. She understands that the porch-sitters' reaction to the Tyler-Who Flung narrative, along with the "envy they had stored up from other times" (2), makes them a hostile audience, to say the least. So Janie quickly dismisses Phoebe's suggestion that she tell them what happened: "Ah don't mean to bother wid tellin' 'em nothin', Pheoby. 'Tain't worth the trouble," she says (6). She then reconsiders and allows Pheoby to tell them her story if she wishes, saying, "You can tell 'em what Ah say if you wants to. Dat's just de same as me 'cause mah tongue is in mah friend's mouf" (6). Just as Ong argues that the examination of a tale's listener can signal the way an author hopes his or her readers will respond, Janie's saying here that her tongue is in her friend's mouth shows her confidence in Pheoby-as-listener's ability to retell the tale. In other words, she likes the idea of Pheoby-the-teller as *model* for the porch-sitters. "[M]ah tongue is in mah friend's mouf" is another way of saying Janie trusts Phoebe's interpretation, her eventual *re*presentation of Janie's tale to the others; the reaction she expects from Pheoby will be the one she would like to see taken to the porch–since she is acutely aware of Phoebe's relationship with the porch-sitters.

But in no way is she actively courting the porch audience. Janie repeatedly and emphatically expresses her disdain for the porch-sitters. Her reaction to their anticipation of a story is the exact opposite of Annie Tyler's when Tyler returned, and for the exact opposite reason. Janie is not broken; she remains proud. And she is prouder still of her overalls and what they represent, even if their meaning is misinterpreted by the onlookers. In a sense, the manner and context that surrounds Janie's insistence that she doesn't care if Pheoby tells the porch-sitters reinforces her detachment. If she were to insist that Pheoby *not* tell them, it would signal that she *did* care what the porch-sitters think. She does not. She casually allows a retelling–entirely at Phoebe's discretion.

Many Hurston scholars, however, view Janie's tale as one she is consciously transmitting–through Pheoby–to the community at large. Anita M. Vickers, for instance, writes that Janie "call[s] upon Pheoby to repeat her story for the porch sitters":

> The inferences made at the beginning of the novel concerning the true audience of *Their Eyes Were Watching God*–the porch sitters–are now made explicit. Thus, the reader suspects that Janie's narrative was told somewhat self-consciously because she is still, even at the completion of her tale, very much aware of this secondary, hostile audience. Because *she insists* that Pheoby retell the story to the porch sitters, one may assume that Janie will become part of the Eatonville folklore; her story will be told, retold and retold once more. . . . She has selflessly relinquished the possession of her vision; it now belongs to the community, an oral art form from which to share and from which to learn. (emphasis mine)[17]

Cathy Bingham, in "The Talking Frame of Zora Neale Hurston's Talking Book: Storytelling as Dialectic in *Their Eyes Were Watching God*," concludes, "At the novel's close, the celebration of orality in which Joe Starks had 'forbidden [Janie] to indulge' (50) is now the shared province of Eatonville's male and female residents. With the device of the talking frame, Hurston affirms Janie's speakerly subjectivity and creates an egalitarian discourse community that finds its voice and its audience in traditional residually oral forms."[18] Elizabeth Meese likewise contends that "Janie returns as a 'speaking subject' to bring her story to the people."[19] Michael Awkward concurs, saying, "Janie seems to assume the role of the prophet. In this role, she wishes to share with people her hard-won knowledge of the world" (54).

Scholars who view Janie as a "prophet" are not taking into account the critical discussion of audience–as demonstrated by the porch-sitters' reaction to the Tyler-Who Flung narrative–that dominates the open and close frames.

Awkward, for instance, mutes the importance of the open frame—and Janie's skeptical, almost dismissive comments about audience—by stating that "because of her own experiences with the masses" she "cannot relate her text personally" (54). However, the text makes it very clear that Janie *refuses* to tell her tale to the community, saying, "If God don't think no mo' 'bout 'em then Ah do, they's a lost ball in de high grass" (5). As Hazel Carby writes, "Janie's definite refusal to tell her tale directly, as in a folktale, distinguishes not only her story from other stories that are communally shared, but also her position from that of the folk as community" (84). In fact, Janie does not enlist the aid of Pheoby to tell the community because, although she doesn't mind Pheoby telling the porch-sitters her story, they are not the audience she has in mind. She wants to—and does—tell the tale to her "friends." Janie's stance allows Hurston to critique the very nature of audience receptivity. Janie's stance employs the audience analysis skills she develops and exercises throughout the novel as she masters the storytelling aesthetic—she ultimately provides the readership with a model for *how to listen* to a tale.

Hurston continues this audience critique when Janie demonstrates her ambivalence toward the community in the close frame. When Pheoby says, "Nobody better not criticize yuh in mah hearin'," Janie responds by saying, in effect, Go ahead and tell them, but don't expect too much if you do: "Dem meatskins is *got* tuh rattle tuh make out they's alive. Let 'em consolate they-selves wid talk" (183). This response echoes Janie's attitude toward the porch-sitters in the open frame. While there is a hint of bemused affection in her comments about the "meatskins" talking on the porch, Janie is clearly skeptical about their potential reaction to her tale. Janie's final, novel-ending comments about the porch-sitters are no more enthusiastic than her open frame senti-ments. She harbors no expectation that her inevitable audience will benefit by the telling. Although Kubitschek is by no means alone in viewing Janie as "a female griot" (67), such interpretations don't take into account Hurston's extended discussion of audience in the open and close frame of the novel.

If Janie has a distinct lack of expectations beyond Pheoby-as-listener, how-ever, an intriguing question is raised: why *tell* stories? Hurston discusses story-telling in both *Mules and Men* (1935) and *Dust Tracks on a Road* (1942). In the former, she talks of the "habit" of "men folks"—and "[e]ven the women folks"—to "gather on the store porch of evenings and swap stories." In the folktales she heard as a child "the devil always outsmarted God and . . . that over-noble hero Jack or John . . . outsmarted the devil." As Hurston sees it, "even the Bible was made over to suit our vivid imaginations."[20] The people of Eatonville, she is saying, used storytelling as a pathway to cultural identity. In the introduction to *Talk That Talk: An Anthology of African-American Storytelling*, Gates concurs, giving storytelling a central, interior position in African-American culture:

The stories that we tell ourselves and our children function to order our world, serving to create both a foundation upon which each of us constructs our sense of reality and a filter through which we process each event that confronts us every day. The values that we cherish and wish to preserve, the behavior that we wish to censure, the fears and dread that we can barely confess in ordinary language, the aspirations and goals that we most dearly prize—all of these things are encoded in the stories that each culture invents and preserves for the next generation, stories that, in effect, we live by and *through*. (17)

This passage could serve to encapsulate everything that happens between the telling and receiving of Janie's tale to Pheoby except, perhaps, the section that refers to the invention and preservation for the next generation. Pheoby arguably receives the depth and breadth of Janie's experience from age sixteen (along with childhood flashbacks) to her fortysomething present day. Pheoby listens as Janie "orders her world" and "constructs" her sense of the "reality" of what she's gone through. Put another way, "Janie," writes Meese, "creates her life through language" (44).

But Janie's tale is, ultimately, an *exception* to Gates's formulation of storytelling as a "preserv[ation] for the next generation." There is a connection between Hurston's dismissal of the community in the open and close frame and her break with storytelling tradition. Earlier, I called Janie's tale a "personal narrative." Dégh, in *Narratives in Society*, refers to different types of storytellers who have different roles in society: "Prestigious narrators with large repertoires are the custodians of the community's stock and have a tremendous influence on fellow storytellers within the community. As keepers of ancestral tradition and bold innovators at the same time, they dominate the network of tale conduits keeping tale-circulation alive. They are role models for young disciples, the aspiring storytellers of the next generation" (10-11).

But Janie doesn't hold this position in Eatonville's community—Janie's tale is a personal narrative. Yes, as Dégh contends, "the concept of personal narrative must be limited to a very few exceptions which would be difficult to recognize as a distinct genre." And her argument that the personal narrative cannot be deemed "nontraditional" since "the telling of a personal narrative is a social act, as is any other narration" is correct as well (75). But there is a distinct difference between the social act of storytelling as Janie talks to Pheoby on her back porch, and, say, Sam, Lige and Walter, "the ringleaders of the mule-talkers," telling stories on the general store's *front* porch. The former is confessional and intimate; the latter is an intentionally public "crayon enlargement of life" for the benefit and amusement of the community at large (48).

So why did Janie tell her story? Cultural identity aside, Janie's main reason for telling her personal narrative is stated in the text: "that oldest human longing–self revelation" (6). It is as "kissin'-friend" that Janie allows Pheoby access to her story.[21]

This "kiss and be kissed" sentiment refers to the first half of the novel, when Janie takes pleasure in being a porch-sitter herself, and–Jody's interference notwithstanding–managed to participate in limited audience membership. Her intuitive break with the storytelling tradition of passing on stories occurs as a result of her separation from the critical porch-sitters in the wake of her relationship with Tea Cake. It is intimacy, then, in light of that break, that informs Janie's manipulation of the storytelling aesthetic. Even after she has gone to the muck and back, it is clear that Janie's attitude toward "Mouth-Almighty" has not changed. So it is not surprising that Pheoby alone is chosen to hear Janie's intimate personal narrative. In "'Mah Tongue Is In Mah Friend's Mouf': The Rhetoric of Intimacy and Immensity in *Their Eyes Were Watching God*," Callahan describes Pheoby in glowing terms. She is

> open, both as Janie's friend and as a friend to her story, whatever its gist and whether it confirms or denies her expectations and values. . . . Pheoby is a sympathetic, rigorous audience. Even though she is Janie's 'best friend,' she will not vouch for her story until she has heard it. Were she to do so before Janie's performance, she would abdicate her right to a full, free response. For her, hearing is believing. (122)

It is not, however, a coincidence that Hurston created a listener who had a dual identity. From a storytelling standpoint, Hurston, as she positions Janie's two audiences–friends and porch-sitters–and Phoebe's "double identity" as a member of both, is expressing a much more ambivalent message regarding "telling" to a "community" audience than has been previously argued. One, Janie is telling an intimate story to her friend, Pheoby, in the "kissing, young darkness" (7). Two, although she does allow Pheoby to tell the porch-sitters, she truly doesn't seem to care; and she cautions Pheoby not to expect too much if she decides to tell. Three, she also refers to what Callahan calls "the limits and possibilities of storytelling" (143) when she talks of how "everybody's got tuh . . . find out about livin' fuh theyselves" (183).

Hurston's ambivalence regarding audience is never more apparent than when Pheoby reacts to Janie's finished tale: "'Lawd!' Pheoby breathed out heavily, 'Ah done growed ten feet higher *from jus' listenin' tuh you*, Janie. *Ah ain't satisfied wid mahself no mo'*. Ah means tuh make Sam take me fishin' wid him after this. Nobody better not criticize yuh in mah hearin'" (182-83, emphasis mine). Pheoby is transformed simply from "listenin'" to Janie, altered to the extent that she "ain't satisfied" with herself anymore, a reaction consistent with African-American frame story convention from Frederick Douglass's "The Heroic Slave" (1853) on. The listener is so captivated by a compelling tale that his or her life or position or political stance is critically altered as a result of the telling. Phoebe's response, however, so well within frame text convention, contradicts Janie's views on storytelling and audience:

> "Now, Pheoby, don't feel too mean wid de rest of 'em 'cause dey's parched up from not knowin' things. Dem meatskins is got tuh rattle tuh make out they's alive. Let 'em consolate theyselves wid talk. 'Course, talkin' don't amount tuh uh hill uh beans when yuh can't do nothin' else. And listenin' tuh dat kind uh talk is jus' lak openin' yo' mouth and lettin' de moon shine down yo' throat. It's uh known fact, Pheoby, you got tuh *go* there tuh *know* there. Yo' papa and yo' mama and nobody else can't tell yuh and show yuh. Two things everybody's got tuh do fuh theyselves. They got tuh go tuh God, and they got tuh find out about livin' fuh theyselves." (183)

Meese sees Janie's words as "a new epistemology. . . . Having gone there, you are changed, and the story you have to tell is a different story. The interpretations of the phallocentric hegemony are called into question rather than assumed. This move wrests the control of meaning from a sexist, racist culture and locates the potential for change within the individual" (51). Maria Tai Wolff, while claiming Pheoby "is moved by Janie's talk to enrich her own life,"[22] also reads Janie's tale as an example of the transformative possibilities of Janie's "(hi)story" on the community. But it is just this transformation that Janie warns Pheoby *not* to expect when representing her tale to the community. Indeed, if Janie, in the important passage above, contends that there is little chance of the porch-sitters understanding and accepting her tale because they are "parched up from not knowin' things," then Hurston is, in effect, arguing for an informed, sympathetic audience, like Pheoby and her other (referred to but unnamed) friends.

Janie, of course, has ample opportunity to tell her tale directly to the porch-sitters when she comes back to Eatonville. She doesn't–because her discovery of the storytelling aesthetic has allowed for her knowledge of the mercurial nature of audience. Hurston, then, through the relationship of Janie, the "text", and Pheoby–teller, tale, and listener–interrogates her reading audience by creating a narrator who speaks of tellers and audiences throughout her text. She is, indeed, holding Pheoby up as a model for her readers, as Ong suggests in his theory, but also as a model for *how to listen*, how to perform the role of audience, what to bring to the teller-tale-listener construct.

Pheoby, like many listeners of storytelling events, does bring a dual identity to the "listener" function of the construct (as does Ralph Ellison's Invisible Man, whose experiences listening to Jim Trueblood will be examined in my next chapter), but her management of these identities makes her a successful storylistener. Indeed, after Janie's declaration that the porch-sitters must find out about living for themselves, the narrator writes of a "finished silence," whereupon "for the first time they could hear the wind picking at the pine trees" (183). Both women's thoughts fill the void. Janie thinks of "that room upstairs–her bedroom" (183). Pheoby, however, "think[s] of Sam waiting for her and getting fretful" instead of thinking about the porch-sitters' possible reaction to the tale. When Pheoby "hug[s] Janie real hard and cut[s] the darkness in flight" (183), she demonstrates that her reaction to the tale is not only to feel "ten feet higher" but to focus her attention on what's truly important–herself, her home, her life–instead of catty townspeople sitting on a porch.

Hurston offers Janie as the central character of the interior tale, and she also offers Pheoby as a critically important model for both the porch-sitters inside the text as well as her readers outside the text. Although Hurston is making a statement about the limits of storytelling when the narrator talks of people needing to "find out about livin' fuh theyselves" (183), Janie giving Pheoby permission to retell the story is also an implied endorsement of the potential of that "other" audience to become the sort of listener Pheoby signifies. Although Hurston's text makes clear her doubts about the transformative powers of storytelling, she is, in the last analysis, "fictionalizing" her readers as falling into one of two categories: intimate "friends," who are able to be transformed by a personal narrative of emotional growth; or "Mouth-Almighty" "meatskins" who, although they seemingly believe in gossip such as the Tyler-Who Flung narrative, and appear to "talk" and "can't do nothin' else" (183), may somehow benefit from the story as well. Ultimately, *Their Eyes Were Watching God*, then, becomes a treatise on audience as much as a text about voice. Hurston's careful audience critique assists and emboldens the transformative power of storytelling–and storylistening.

CHAPTER 3

Listening to the Blues
Ralph Ellison's Trueblood Episode in *Invisible Man*

On the front porch of his house, on an unseasonably warm Southern spring day in the middle of the century, Jim Trueblood told a long tale to a young Negro college student and one Mr. Norton, a wealthy donor to the college. Trueblood's tale occupies the majority of chapter two of Ralph Ellison's *Invisible Man*. In Charles Chesnutt's *The Conjure Woman* the short stories are rendered with a textual frame, as is Zora Neale Hurston's *Their Eyes Were Watching God*. Their length differences notwithstanding, in both Chesnutt's and Hurston's texts the relationship between teller and listener inside the text seems to mirror the hoped-for relationship between text and reader. In *Invisible Man*, once again there is an inside-the-text teller and inside-the-text listeners; however, this is an *embedded* narrative rather than a formal "frame" narrative.[1]

Embedded narratives must be considered in the context of the events of a novel that happen before and after the storytelling event. For example, in *Invisible Man*, the Trueblood episode is a distinct text unto itself, but it is also an early "adventure" in Invisible Man's quest to understand himself. "Adventure" is the term Susan Rubin Suleiman uses in *Authoritarian Fictions: The Ideological Novel As a Literary Genre*. She defines a "story of apprentice-ship"[2]

> as two parallel transformations undergone by the protagonist: first, a trans-formation from *ignorance* (of self) to *knowledge* (of self); second, a transfor-mation from *passivity* to *action*. The hero goes forth into the world to find (knowledge of) himself, and attains such knowledge through a series of "adventures" (actions) that function both as "proofs" and as tests. The

adventures in which the hero triumphs are the means whereby he "discovers his own essence"–they thus fulfill the traditional function of a text; but they constitute, at the same time, a "proof" of his new-found knowledge of self, which is the necessary precondition for authentic action in the future. In effect, the hero's "adventures" are but the prelude to genuine action: a story of apprenticeship ends on the threshold of a "new life" for the hero–which explains why, in the traditional *Bildungsroman*, the hero is always a young man, often an adolescent. (65)

Suleiman's "story of apprenticeship" theory describes the actions of the hero of *Invisible Man* from the Battle Royale, his earliest "adventure," through the epilogue, where the demonstration of his "new-found knowledge of self" suggests a "prelude to genuine action." His readiness to emerge from his "hole" at novel's end does signal a "'new life' for the hero."

The Trueblood episode is, indeed, an "adventure" that is vital to the reading of the novel as Invisible Man's growth from a naive college student to a mature, knowledgeable individual. But it is the episode's execution of the blues mode[3] that allows Invisible Man to demonstrate his transformation in the epilogue after his "adventures" pile on top of each other. For both Invisible Man-the-listener and the reader of his autobiography, the episode shows Trueblood as a model of what Invisible Man would become: a bluesman. Mr. Norton, on the other hand, listens differently and emerges as a problematic model for readers who identify with him. Norton, too, makes an appearance in the epilogue. But Invisible Man goes beyond merely providing "the rest of the story" to the Trueblood episode; much as Hurston does in the closing pages of *Their Eyes Were Watching God*, Ellison's narrator discusses the very nature of audience itself. As we shall see, Invisible Man ponders his readers' possible reception of his narrative, and in the process he reveals his "fictionalization" of his readers. His discussion of his intended audience in the epilogue speaks to his models inside the text, and the connection between Trueblood and Invisible Man becomes even more evident when viewed through these novel-ending comments.

Like Ong, Suleiman sees inside-the-text listeners as models for readers. In a discussion of the novel *L'Etape*, Suleiman writes that when one character "reads" the stories of his brother and sister, he "occupies a position analogous to that of the reader of their stories and of the novel as a whole. His act of interpretation is a mimesis of the general activity of the reader–and the consequence of this interpretation, which is a change in his whole way of being and acting, is also presumably supposed to function as a model, or as a mirror image, for the reader" (79). As we have seen in Hurston's novel, where Pheoby acts as model for both the porch-sitters and the readership, Ellison, in his "Working Notes for *Invisible Man*," envisions Trueblood as a model for the narrator:

> Against the tragic-comic attitude adopted by folk Negroes (best expressed by the blues and in our scheme by Trueblood) [Invisible Man] is strictly, during the first phase of his life, of the nineteenth century. Thus neither he nor Mr. Norton, whose abolitionist father's creation he is, can respond to Trueblood's stoicism, or to the Vet's need to get close to the naked essence of the world as he has come to see it. Life is either tragic or absurd, but Norton and the boy have no capacity to deal with such ambivalence. The boy would appease the gods; it costs him much to discover that he can satisfy the gods only by rebelling against them. (344)

Ellison holds Trueblood up as an example of a stoic bluesman who adopts a tragic-comic attitude to grapple with the absurdities of African-American life.[4] And when Ellison provides Trueblood as an additional "invisible man"–one who, "when they approach [him] they see only [his] surroundings, themselves, or figments of their imagination–indeed, everything and anything except"[5] the individual that Trueblood truly is–Ellison also imbues Trueblood with a stoicism that outlasts and transcends the obstacles placed before him.[6] The early "point" to the novel's latter "counterpoint," then, is made through storytelling. Trueblood is, according to Robert Stepto, a "master storyteller."[7] Invisible Man writes that Trueblood "told the old stories with a sense of humor and a magic that made them come alive" (46). And through his storytelling, Trueblood embodies what Henry Louis Gates, Jr. calls "the improvisatory prehistory of the blues."[8]

Trueblood tells his tale to a double audience–literally, he repeatedly tells the tale to both black and white audiences. These storytelling events constitute Trueblood's "adventures," in the Suleiman sense, and they prefigure Invisible Man's "adventures" as well. The first telling happens the morning after the incident, when Kate, after leaving the house to go down the road, "comes back with some women to see 'bout Matty Lou. Won't nobody speak to me," says Trueblood, "though they looks at me like I'm some new kinda cottonpickin' machine. I feels bad. I tells them how it happened in a dream, but they scorns me" (65-6). After that first futile telling, Trueblood "goes to see the preacher and even he don't believe me. He tells me to git out of his house, that I'm the most wicked man he's ever seen and that I better go confess my sin and make my peace with God" (66). As a result of telling his stories, Trueblood undergoes a transformation, as will Invisible Man much later. At the preacher's behest, Trueblood goes off to be alone with God. This religious retreat includes fasting and denial of fluids, until the transcendence of the blues intervene:

> I leaves tryin' to pray, but I caint. I thinks and thinks, until I thinks my brain is go'n bust, 'bout how I'm guilty and how I ain't guilty. I don't eat nothin' and I don't drink nothin' and I caint sleep at night. Finally one night, way early in the mornin', I looks up and sees the stars and I starts singin'. I don't

mean to, I didn't think 'bout it, just start singin'. I don't know what it was, some kinda church song, I guess. All I know is I *ends up* singin' the blues. I sings me some blues that night ain't never been sang before, and while I'm singin' them blues I makes up my mind that I ain't nobody but myself and ain't nothin' I can do but let whatever is gonna happen, happen. (66)

Before Trueblood's retreat, his storytelling attempts were futile, and he was frustrated by his audiences' refusal to believe his tale.[9] After the retreat, however, where Trueblood "makes up [his] mind," the reaction to his tale differs somewhat. He still gets an understandably negative reaction when he next "tells Kate and Matty Lou 'bout the dream" (66), but when Kate's first words are "How come you don't go on 'way and leave us?," Trueblood reacts by saying, "I'm a man and a man don't leave his family" (66).

The retreat thus provides the tale with a turning point, a point that occurs with Trueblood's singing of the blues. The movement from religious to secular, from singing a church song that "*ends up* [with] singin' the blues," signals Trueblood's transformation from what Ellison calls a "pre-individualistic state" to that of being an individual who does what he feels he must. As Houston Baker, Jr. writes, "The first unpremeditated expression that Trueblood summons is a religious song. But the religious system that gives birth to the song is, presumably, one in which the term "incest" carries pejorative force. Hence, the sharecropper moves on, spontaneously, to the blues" (187-88).

The three specific black audiences he talks to (the women taking care of Kate, the preacher, and Kate and Mattie) all react negatively to his tale. He finds more rejection when he tells the tale to other blacks, including those at the school, who are, perhaps, most hostile to Trueblood and his act. They offer to send Trueblood and his family out of the county, but Trueblood refuses, and an interesting power play develops as a result of his refusal: both Trueblood and the "biggety school folks" use the threat of white influence as instruments of power in order to get their way. In a scene somewhat reminiscent of Chloe's going to her slavemaster to get satisfaction from Hannibal's autonomous revenge plot in Chesnutt's "Hot-Foot Hannibal," the school officials threaten to "turn the white folks loose on" Trueblood. Trueblood admits that "Them folks up there to the school is in strong with the white folks and that scared me" (52), but after they call him a "disgrace" he "got real mad [and] went down to see Mr. Buchanan, the boss man. . ." (52).

He then begins to tell his tale to whites, with much more "positive" results than he has with his earlier black audiences. He moves from Buchanan to Sheriff Barbour, who, in turn, "called in some more men" to hear it again. "They wanted to hear about the gal lots of times and they gimme somethin' to eat and drink and some tobacco" says Trueblood. "Surprised me, 'cause I was scared and spectin' somethin' different. Why I guess there ain't a colored man in the county who ever got to take so much of the white folkses time as I did" (53). The revelation that he was "scared" telling his tale to whites echoes the way he was "scared" when the blacks from the school threatened to exercise their influence with powerful whites. Obviously, however, he was willing to tell the whites himself because he was either less afraid of white reaction than he was of the school administrators' connection with whites, or because, regardless of what happened, he insisted on retaining agency and carrying the message himself. More than likely it was a combination of both.

At bottom, his white audience's reaction to his tale is astonishingly different from the black reaction:

> [T]he white folks took to coming out here to see us and talk with us. Some of 'em was big white folks, too, from the big school way cross the State. Asked me lots 'bout what I thought 'bout things, and 'bout my folks and the kids, and wrote it all down in a book. (53)

It would be a mistake, however, to assume that Trueblood's repeated tale is told virtually verbatim at each telling. Baker writes that the

> multiple narrative frames and voices in Ellison's Trueblood episode include the novel Invisible Man, the protagonist's fictive autobiographical account, Norton's story recalled as part of the fictive autobiography, Trueblood's story as framed by the fictive autobiography, the sharecropper's own autobiographical recall, the dream narrative within that autobiographical recall. All these stories reflect, or 'objectify,' one another in ways that complicate their individual and composite meanings. (176)

But when Trueblood tells his tale to the different facets of the black community, "the tale" is actually Trueblood talking about "the dream" in an effort to explain how it is that he managed to impregnate both his daughter and his wife at approximately the same time. By the time he tells the tale to Norton and Invisible Man, he is talking about the dream *and the aftermath* to explain not just how they became pregnant but how his life has changed in the interim. As such, it is important to note that the tale Trueblood tells to the women, to the preacher, and to Kate and Matty Lou is not the same tale Invisible Man records in his memoir. The tale he tells to the whites, on the other hand, has expanded to a discussion of the night it happened, the economic context of that night's winter, his state of mind *regarding* the economic context of that winter, the dream, and the incest act itself.[10]

Trueblood, master storyteller that he is, shapes and adapts his story to his audience. Still, the difference between white reaction and black reaction is something that does not get past Trueblood, even as he claims not to understand it:

Things got to happenin' right off. The nigguhs up at the school come down
to chase me off and that made me mad. That's what I don't understand. I done
the worse thing a man could ever do in his family and instead of chasin' me
out of the country, [whites] gimme more help than they ever give any other
colored man, no matter how good a nigguh he was. Except that my wife an'
daughter won't speak to me, I'm better off than I ever been before. (67)

Trueblood reveals the various audience reactions to his tale over the eight-plus
months since the incident itself, and they mirror the white/black reaction to
the audience before him as he sits and talks to Invisible Man and Mr. Norton.

Indeed, Mr. Norton brings all of the contradictions, confusions, and, perhaps above all, *guilt* of the paternalistic white aristocracy to his hearing of the
tale. As Ellison makes clear in his "Notes," Trueblood is not speaking to an
audience that can "respond" when he tells his tale to Mr. Norton and Invisible
Man. Recall that Ellison asserts that "Norton and the boy have no capacity to
deal with such ambivalence" (344). Invisible Man describes Norton as a "mul-
timillionaire," with "A face pink like St. Nicholas' topped with a shock of silk
white hair. An easy, informal manner. . . . A Bostonian, smoker of cigars, teller
of polite Negro stories, shrewd banker, skilled scientist, director, philanthro-
pist, forty years a bearer of the white man's burden, and for sixty a symbol of
the Great Traditions" (37).

Co-listener Invisible Man, however, is by turns ashamed, disgusted, and
embarrassed because he is (still) trapped in his double-consciousness: he sees
Trueblood through Mr. Norton's eyes. Wolfgang Iser writes, "The traditional
hero of the novel is endowed with a quite specific function: he is the focal
point of reference for virtually all events in the world he represents, and he
gives the reader the opportunity to participate in these events."[11] So it is important that Invisible Man, early in chapter two, writes of Mr. Norton, "I felt that
I was sharing in a great work and, with the car leaping leisurely beneath the
pressure of my foot, I *identified myself* with the rich man reminiscing on the
rear seat. . ." (39, italics added). Mr. Norton, in fact, becomes the "focal point"
for "virtually all [of the] events" that follow in the chapter.

It is in connection with his "fate" that Invisible Man identifies with Mr.
Norton; importantly, his lack of identification with Trueblood extends further
narrative identification to Mr. Norton. This identification is important since, as
I will discuss below, Invisible Man revisits his relationship with Mr. Norton in
the epilogue, after the bulk of his narrative has been related and after he has
come to understand and reconcile his double consciousness. At this early
stage, however, the reader can only "read" Invisible Man by paying attention
to his comments about the way the school administrators view Trueblood.
The school officials called Trueblood's music "primitive spirituals" (47).
Invisible Man adds, "We were embarrassed by the earthy harmonies they sang,

but since the visitors were awed we dared not laugh at the crude, high, plain-tively animal sounds Jim Trueblood made as he led the quartet" (47). These statements are further examples of the difference between the black audience and the white audience's possible reception of Trueblood's performance–both musical *and* storytelling. Whenever the black middle class (signified in this instance by Invisible Man, the rest of the students, and the school's officials) is confronted with an example of black folk expression, it blanches.

For Trueblood's tale is spliced with comments by Invisible Man that speak to his discomfort in the white gaze, to his "sense of shame" (68) at hearing Trueblood's sometimes ribald narrative in the presence of a white person: "How can he tell this to white men, I thought, when he knows they'll say that all Negroes do such things?" (58). (This question is a precursor to a question Invisible Man would ask himself much later in the novel. Just as Invisible Man asks himself why Trueblood would tell his tale to Mr. Norton, he later asks himself why, indeed, he would tell his own tale [579].) In his "Notes," Ellison sees Trueblood's "stoicism" and the Vet's pursuit of "the naked essence of the world" as values to be emulated; he makes it clear that Invisible Man, at least early on, and Norton have "no capacity" to "deal with such ambivalence." Ellison's "Notes" position Trueblood and the Vet as legitimate polar opposites of Norton and "the boy," emphasizing that Norton is a product of a socioe-conomic climate that doesn't demand that he grapple with the "absurd predicament" in which Negroes find themselves. Invisible Man, however, as Ellison states, "represents the Negro individualist, the personality that breaks away from the pre-individual community of southern Negro life to win its way in the jim crow world by guile, uncletomming, or ruthlessness. In order to do this he must act within the absurd predicament in which Negroes find them-selves upon the assumption that all is completely logical" (344).

Invisible Man has, by narrative's end, achieved some semblance of individ-uality. There are two instances in the second chapter, shortly before Trueblood tells his tale, that remind the reader that Invisible Man is recalling these events and interpreting them from the individualist stance he has achieved by the end of the narrative.[12] These two moments help ground the events in the correct time. The first reference point occurs when Mr. Norton hands his daughter's miniature to Invisible Man. "She was very beautiful, I thought *at the time*. . .," he writes. "I know *now* that it was the flowing costume of soft, flimsy material that made for the effect; *today* . . . she would appear as ordinary as an expensive piece of machine-tooled jewelry and just as lifeless. *Then*, however," he concludes, "I shared something of his enthusiasm" (43 italics added). The juxtaposition of "at the time" and "now," and of "today" and "then," emphasizes the fact that Invisible Man-the-character shares duties with Invisible Man-the-narrator. The character serves the narrator's ideological ends, and this short reference to time reminds the reader that this is not simply the telling of a linear story but the recounting of a series of events that is being interpreted from the perspective of a man who has come to understand his invisibility.

This brief reminder of the narrator's perspective remains a momentary pause in the narrator's concentration on Invisible Man's school experiences until the narrator pauses again in the midst of relating how the college's inhabitants were embarrassed by Jim Trueblood as he led the quartet. When Invisible Man writes, "That had all passed now with his disgrace," the word "now," no longer means as-I-sit-in-my-basement; it refers to the episode-specific time when Trueblood was no longer welcome at the school after impregnating his wife and daughter. But the next sentence again situates the narrator underground, as he clearly marks the difference between the present and the past he writes about: "I didn't understand in those pre-invisible days that their hate, and mine too, was charged with fear" (47). Further, Invisible Man uses this additional time-shift-reference to comment on how much he's learned in between the past and the present-day writing of his autobiography. He also refers to a nonspecific "we" that could be taken more than one way: "How all of us at the college hated the black-belt people, the 'peasants,' during those days! We were trying to lift them up and they, like Trueblood, did everything it seemed to pull them down" (47).

This reference to "those days" is relayed in first person plural. He could simply be referring to "us" because of the obvious fact there were a plurality of students at the school. However, that sentence could also possibly hint that what Invisible Man has undergone in between the time he spent at school and the writing of the narrative in his room is a transformation in how he views the black folk, the "peasants." The first person plural point of view could, additionally, speak to a hoped-for massive, class-crossing alteration of how African-Americans deal with "the absurd predicament" in which they find themselves upon assuming that "all is completely logical" (344), given that Trueblood and the Vet are mature bluesmen.

I read the Trueblood episode as a way for Ellison to suggest to black middle class readers an alternative reaction to the Truebloods—and the Mr. Nortons—of America. And white readers who have, for reasons I discuss above, identified with Mr. Norton, can see how far they have *not* come.[13] My sense is that Ellison inserted these two time-shift reminders so that when Invisible Man returns to real time in the epilogue the readers (black and white) can see how far he's come, and how far they, as readers, may have come as well. Through the same process of identification, at the end of the novel, the black middle class could glimpse the idea of a progression of their own.

This second time-reference also suggests that the Trueblood episode is, in fact, incomplete as an episode in and of itself, that it is actually a crucial set-up that will show the reader the contrast between a naive Invisible Man and the Invisible Man who has grown into the realization that all is not "completely logical." The reader, as a result of watching and hearing Trueblood-the-model's "stoicism" in action, can begin to glimpse the transformation Invisible Man has gone through by the time the epilogue appears. The critical moment in that epilogue, for the purposes of this discussion, comes when Invisible Man recalls seeing Mr. Norton in the subway:

> He's lost, I thought, and he'll keep coming until he sees me, then he'll ask for direction. Maybe there's an embarrassment in it if he admits he's lost to a strange white man. Perhaps to lose a sense of *where* you are implies the danger of losing a sense of *who* you are. That must be it, I thought—to lose your direction is to lose your face. So here he comes to ask his direction from the lost, the invisible. Very well, I've learned to live without direction. Let him ask. (577)

Over the course of the novel, Invisible Man has come to recognize his invisibility, and as a result he has learned to "live without direction." But here he implies that Mr. Norton has also lost a sense of who he is during his absence from the real time of the novel.

In fact, Invisible Man, as his "adventures" pass one after the other, has himself come to realize the critical "loss" of those who deny the richness of black contributions to American culture. Gates, in a profile of Albert Murray, called Ellison's insistence on a black core to the American way of life as "perhaps the most breathtaking act of cultural chutzpa this land had witnessed since Columbus blithely claimed it all for Isabella":

> In its bluntest form, [Murray and Ellison's] assertion was that the truest Americans were black Americans. For much of what was truly distinctive about America's "national character" was rooted in the improvisatory pre-history of the blues. The very sound of American English "is derived from the timbre of the African voice and the listening habits of the African ear," Ellison maintained. "If there is such a thing as a Yale accent, there is a Negro wail in it." (76)

In James Alan McPherson's "Indivisible Man," Ellison says emphatically, "I recognize no American culture which is not the partial creation of black people. I recognize no American style in literature, in dance, in music, even in assembly-line processes, which does not bear the mark of the American Negro" (*Collected Essays* 356).

Ellison, in *Invisible Man*, prefigures his non-fiction writings that confirm African-Americans' place at the center of American culture. "But I'm your destiny," says Invisible Man to Mr. Norton in the epilogue, "I made you. Why shouldn't I know you?" He goes on to suggest that Norton "Take any train; they all go to the Golden D[ay]" (578), metaphorically implying that the totality of American culture is inextricably entwined with African-American life and folkways. If some white readers were identifying with Mr. Norton during the Trueblood episode, the assumption here is that those whites have, as well, lost a sense of who they are since they don't realize their "black" cultural roots. Ellison says as much in the closing pages of the novel:

> America is woven of many strands; I would recognize them and let it so remain. It's "winner take nothing" that is the great truth of our country or of any country. Life is to be lived, not controlled; and humanity is won by continuing to play in the face of certain defeat. Our fate is to become one, and yet many–This is not prophecy but description. Thus one of the greatest jokes in the world is the spectacle of the whites busy escaping blackness and becoming blacker every day, and the blacks striving towards whiteness, and becoming quite dull and gray. (577)

It is this intercultural comment that prompts Invisible Man to a recollection of Norton. Invisible Man, then, effectively turns Norton's chapter two statement ("you are involved in my life quite intimately, even though you've never seen me before. You are bound to a great dream and to a beautiful monument" [43]), into an example of how far Invisible Man has come since then. When first uttered, the words confuse Invisible Man because he still identified with Norton. Now he is clear about its meaning. Norton, in the earlier chapter, makes a paternal reference to his "first-hand organizing of human life" (42). But by the end of the narrative, Invisible Man understands that it is the influence of the American Negro which has, in part, influenced Norton. By taking Norton's comments and turning them on their head, Invisible Man exhibits the combination of white-black culture that accurately reflects the history between blacks and whites in this country.

But the novel-ending meeting between Norton and Invisible Man does far more than that. It re-contextualizes the Trueblood episode, modulating and expanding it in a fashion that frame texts such as Chesnutt's and Hurston's can only accomplish by projecting beyond the text. *Invisible Man* provides a storytelling event in the second chapter and then allows its readers the rest of the book to view its results.

The embedded narrative allows readers to glimpse a tangible growth process as the novel plays out. As the readers–white and black, with their myriad patterns of identification–read on to witness Invisible Man grappling with the Brotherhood and Lucius Brockway, Mary Rambo and Ras the Destroyer, even Rinehart, the possibility exists that their worldview will be altered. The early-on Trueblood episode and the book-ending reprisal of the Norton-Invisible Man connection highlight this possible growth.

However, Invisible Man puzzles with the idea of exactly who his audience is in the closing pages of the book. The closing five paragraphs of the novel, beginning with "So why do I write, torturing myself to put it down?" (579) to the last, one-sentence paragraph that ends the book, "Who knows but that, on the lower frequencies, I speak for you?" (581), address the notion of audience—in effect, he discusses who he means by "you," even though he never explicitly says so. Michel Fabre, in "The Narrator/Narratee Relationship in *Invisible Man*," makes a compelling case for the narratee, or the "fictional construct [who] should not be confused with the actual reader,"[14] being "a member of the white West" (541). Fabre bases his conclusion on Ellison's use of the narratee-addressed "you," reading closely for clues as to whether Ellison belongs to the addressed group or not.

> That the novel does address itself to white America is made clear in other, equally important sections of the Epilogue. During the last attempt at interpreting the grandfather's riddle . . . the narrator asks: "Did he mean to affirm the principle which they themselves (i.e., the men who did the violence) . . . had violated . . . ? Or did he mean that we had to take the responsibility for all of it . . . because we, with the given circumstances of our origin, could only thus find transcendence?" (574). This sounds like an inner monologue in response to the grandfather's question, not like an address to the reader, but it clearly identifies "they" as the racists, the white American oppressors, and "we" as the Black community. (542)

Here Fabre selects an excerpt that does more than suggest whites as the audience. This passage suggests that while the narrative might be *addressed* to white readers, it *assumes* black readers as well. Otherwise, the above question containing the "we" has no one to ponder an answer. This stance–the familiar difficulty of the dual-audience–is yet another quandary that Invisible Man must overcome.

The audience discussion hinges upon the position Invisible Man takes when he wishes to "at least *tell* a few people about" his experiences (579), even as he imagines he knows how the (white) reader will react: "'Ah,' I can hear you say, 'so it was all a build-up to bore us with his buggy jiving. He only wanted us to listen to him rave!'" (581). Through his narrator, at the end of his novel, Ellison is wrestling with one of the chief conundrums of the African-American artist: how to communicate with an audience that would "refuse to see me. . . . [T]hey see only my surroundings, themselves, or figments of their imagination–indeed, everything and anything except me" (3). Invisible Man sees the problem, and its tenable solution, this way:

> The very act of trying to put it all down has confused me and negated some of the anger and some of the bitterness. So it is that now I denounce and defend, or feel prepared to defend. I condemn and affirm, say no and say yes, say yes and say no. I denounce because though implicated and partially

responsible, I have been hurt to the point of abysmal pain, hurt to the point of invisibility. And I defend because in spite of all I find that I love. In order to get some of it down I *have* to love. I sell you no phony forgiveness, I'm a desperate man—but too much of your life will be lost, its meaning lost, unless you approach it as much through love as through hate. So I approach it through division. So I denounce and I defend and I hate and I love. (579-80)

With this statement, Invisible Man demonstrates that he has adopted the blues mode; he has, through great trial and error, attained Trueblood's sense that, having found himself "in a tight spot like that there," trying to figure a way "to git myself out of the fix I'm in," he had to "move without movin'" (59). Baker writes, "If desire and absence are driving conditions of blues performance, the amelioration of such conditions is implied by the onomatopoeic *training* of blues voice and instrument. Only a *trained* voice can sing the blues" (8). Baker's pun is obvious, as Invisible Man has been properly "trained," over the length of the novel to sing the blues. John S. Wright puts it this way:

> Rinehart and Trueblood are ultimately the *non*political poles of sensibility between which the narrator must mediate his own ambiguous sense of freedom as necessity *and* as possibility. Despite Rinehart's unmediated freedom and Trueblood's subjection to psychic and social necessity, what Rinehart and Trueblood share is their existential awareness that to be free one must be able to "move without moving," a problem that Rinehart *masters* but Trueblood *transcends*.[15]

Although Ellison's "Notes" are undated and are thought to have been written sometime "after beginning *Invisible Man* in 1945" (*Collected Essays* 341), they speak to Invisible Man's dilemma as if, perhaps, the end of the novel had not yet been written when the "Notes" were composed. Invisible Man has come to understand that the problem of how to figure an unfigureable audience will be solved (as much as it can be solved) only if he can "approach it through division." This contrast between the naive and mature Invisible Man provides a completion to the Trueblood episode; Invisible Man can now "sing the blues" as well as Trueblood can. His hard-fought ability to adopt the ambiguous "tragic-comic attitude adopted by folk Negroes" complements Trueblood's example of the same much earlier in the novel. As Invisible Man puts it late in the book, "in spite of myself I've learned some things" (579).

This narrative, then, in a sense, functions the same way Trueblood's ritualistic fast-turned-prayer-turned-church-song-turned-singin'-the-blues moment that moves his tale from tragic to transcendent. Recall that Trueblood says then, "All I know is I *ends up* singing' the blues. I sings me some blues that night ain't never been sang before, and while I'm singin' them blues I makes up my mind that I ain't nobody but myself and ain't nothin' I can do but let whatever is gonna happen, happen. I made up my mind. . ." (66). This decisive moment that literally grows out of the blues mirrors this equally transcendent moment in the epilogue of *Invisible Man*:

> So now having tried to put it down I have disarmed myself in the process. You won't believe in my invisibility and you'll fail to see how any principle that applies to you could apply to me. You'll fail to see it even though death waits for both of us if you don't. Nevertheless, the very disarmament has brought me to a decision. The hibernation is over. (580)

And he readies himself to come out with full knowledge of the ambiguity he carries, saying, "invisibility has taught my nose to classify. . ." (580). While "there's still a conflict within me," he writes, "a decision has been made. I'm shaking off the old skin, and I'll leave it in the hole. I'm coming out, no less invisible without it, but coming out nevertheless" (581). Perhaps it is the word "nevertheless," both here and above, that speaks to the growth of Invisible Man. His ability to exist with ambiguity is now his strength.

This ambiguity-as-strength is what he utilizes as he speaks to the "you" in his text, a "you" I, too, read as referring to white Americans. When he projects his (white) readers as thinking "Ah, . . . so it was all a build-up to bore us with his buggy jiving. He only wanted us to listen to him rave!," he responds that such a reaction would only be "partially true" and concludes, "Being invisible and without substance, a disembodied voice, as it were, what else could I do? What else but try to tell you what was really happening when your eyes were looking through?" (581). He is saying he had no choice, that the events of the narrative were what he *could* do. In Trueblood's words, he is now determined to "let whatever is gonna happen, happen."

As such, the Trueblood episode, even though it is an embedded narrative rather than a frame narrative, cements the idea of the frame acting as model. The difference here is that the rest of the novel acts as a "close frame"; the Trueblood episode is unintelligible without it.

CHAPTER 4

The Best "Possible Returns"

Storytelling and Gender Relations in
James Alan McPherson's "The Story of a Scar"

Since Dr. Wayland was late and there were no recent newsmagazines in the
waiting room, I turned to the other patient and said: "As a concerned person,
and as your brother, I ask you, without meaning to offend, how did you get
that scar on the side of your face?"

The woman seemed insulted. Her brown eyes, which before had been wan-
dering vacuously about the room, narrowed suddenly and sparked humbling
reprimands at me. She took a draw on her cigarette, puckered her lips, and
blew a healthy stream of smoke toward my face. It was a mean action, deliberately irreverent and cold. The long curving scar on her face darkened. "I ask
you, as a nosy person with no connections in your family, how come your
nose is all bandaged up?"[1]

It's a standoff. Both waiting room inhabitants in James Alan McPherson's
"The Story of a Scar" are in need of medical attention; both are curious about
the other's injury; and both either use or refute the general use of the terms
"brother" and "sister" to address African-Americans. This tit-for-tat repartee
between total strangers, one an African-American man and one an African-
American woman, begins the interaction between them. By the end of the
story, their relationship has provided an illustration of what Orlando
Patterson calls "a crisis in nearly all aspects of gender relations among all
classes of Afro-Americans."[2]

"From time to time," writes Patterson in *Rituals of Blood: Consequences of
Slavery in Two American Centuries*, "the issue bursts on the scene in sudden
gusts of very angry talk usually stimulated by some artistic or literary event"
(4). During the late seventies, it was Ntozake Shange's play *for colored girls who
have considered suicide/when the rainbow is enuf* (1977) and Michele Wallace's

book *Black Macho and the Myth of the Superwoman* (1978) that prompted a heated discussion of black gender relations. The Broadway run of *for colored girls...* and the wide reception of *Black Macho* prompted a black male response, including Robert Staples's "The Myth of Black Macho: A Response to Angry Black Feminists" in the March-April 1979 issue of *The Black Scholar*, as well as a special collection of articles on "Black Male/Female Relationships" in *The Black Scholar*'s following issue. But McPherson avoids polarities in "The Story of a Scar," published in *Elbow Room*, his 1977 Pulitzer Prize-winning collection of stories. Like Toni Cade Bambara's "My Man Bovanne," McPherson's treatment of these two characters, particularly the narrator, explores one of the signal black issues of the era.

After all, finding out what happened to the teller's face essentially comes in third on the narrator's list of priorities above. Certainly, he would prefer to have his nose bandages taken off immediately; that's why he's at the office. But his ranking of "recent newsmagazines" as second in importance makes his solemn "concern" for the teller sound suspect. And her suspicion is well-founded, as it turns out. As we shall see, the narrator carries certain assumptions about what–and who–could have caused the woman's face to be scarred; for her part, her suspicion causes her to react the way she does. She is "offend[ed]" by his question, she responds accordingly, and the chief conflict of the outer frame is underway.

As such, the open frame of "The Story of a Scar" does what we have seen open frames do in Charles W. Chesnutt's dialect tales, Zora Neale Hurston's *Their Eyes Were Watching God*, and Ralph Ellison's *Invisible Man*: it contextualizes the story, establishes the main themes, introduces the reader to the teller and the listener, and informs the reader of the stakes for both teller and listener. And as the above epigraph makes clear, there is, initially, very little at stake for the narrator/listener. There is, however, much at stake for what Robert Stepto calls the "discourse of distrust."[3] Stepto does define a "basic written tale" as "a framed tale in which either the framed or framing narrative depicts a black storyteller's white listener socially and morally maturing into competency" (207). But Stepto also repeatedly refers to incompetent black listeners, as well. He describes Richard Wright, for instance, as having had to "learn how to perform . . . before unreliable audiences, white and black," and suggests that Wright wrote *Uncle Tom's Children* so that he could "appease the distrust he encountered from blacks and whites" once he came North (197).

As the Trueblood episode of *Invisible Man* makes obvious, a black teller's distrust isn't immediately "suspended" simply because his or her listener is black. Patterson reports,

> In a study of 256 mainly working- and lower-middle-class Afro-American students at Temple University, Noel Cazenave and Rita Smith asked respon-

dents for their views on Michele Wallace's assertion that there was "distrust, even hatred, between black men and women." Only 34 percent of the men, and 26 percent of the women disagreed with this statement. . . . And Castellano Turner and Barbara Turner, in their study of Afro-American evaluations of future marital relations, found that most Afro-American women considered "most men" less responsible, reliable, trustworthy, and happy. While most Afro-American men considered Afro-American women "trustworthy," the researchers were forced to conclude that "black females' views of relationships with black men were laced with the anticipation of disappointment." (5)

The two black patients in Dr. Wayland's waiting room fit this description. From their contentious beginning, the female teller and the listener/narrator quickly develop a mutually distrustful, if not mutually antagonistic storytelling relationship. And at the heart of the teller's tale is her difficult and damaging relationship with her former boyfriend, Billy Crawford, whom she met and came to know as both worked at a U.S. postal office. Their relationship was made all the more trying because of the hostility their pairing prompted from the rest of the African-Americans who worked there. The narrative explores what Patricia Hill Collins calls "the tensions between African-American men and women"[4] through an extended, combative storytelling event.

Much of the difficulty between this storyteller and this listener stem from the narrator's preexisting assumptions, a situation that is not uncommon in the written representation of oral storytelling.[5] This narrator displays both his assumptions and the reason for the teller's distrust as he secretly opens what I call "narrative negotiations" between the two of them. The negotiating advantage appears, early on, to be with the narrator. When the scarred woman asks why his nose is bandaged up, he confides to his readers—but not, obviously, the woman—"It was a fair question, considering the possible returns on its answer" (97). The "returns" he receives is the tale she tells. When he explains that he "smashed [his nose] against the headboard of [his] bed while engaged in the act of love," she laughs uproariously. He writes, "Her appetites were whetted. She looked me up and down, almost approvingly, and laughed some more. . ." (97-8). But his baldly obvious negotiating ploy does inform the "crisis" mentality to which Patterson refers. The narrator coldly answers the woman's question as an *investment*, hoping he can subsequently cash in with a story.

And he does. His investment pays off. She tells her tale. But he also gets more than he "bargained" for, because her tale, in form and content, isn't at all what he expected. For her part, the female patient struggles for agency. She insists on telling her tale her way. The narrator, for his part, constantly interrupts and even attempts to preempt her tale as she tells it. To an extent, his interruptions have to do with time. The story takes place in a Northern, urban "surgeon's office" (98) where time matters–unlike, say, a freedman telling his employer a tale during a lazy Sunday on a piazza in the South. Even though the actual storytelling event doesn't take place on the street, the strict emphasis on time effectively ushers the hustle and bustle of city life into the waiting room; this is a necessarily terse encounter, since Dr. Wayland's arrival could end the tale at any moment.

Although time concerns don't fully explain the narrator's behavior, it is a critical part of the context of the tale. Storytelling time, like baseball time or barbershop time, is not fixed. It's elastic, with its own time markers. Baseball games are marked by innings, barbershop visits are marked by haircuts, and both of these time markers can vary greatly on the way to completion. This particular storytelling event is not marked by hours, minutes, or seconds–it's marked by cigarettes. The teller languorously smokes three cigarettes during the course of the narrative. Recall that she is smoking the first cigarette as the narrator asks his opening question, and she deliberately blows "a healthy stream of smoke" directly into his face (98). And while the action does more to illustrate the tension between these patients, the action is also the first of three distinct nonverbal moments marked by the teller's smoking and handling of cigarettes: the open frame, the tale itself, and the close frame.

During an early, silent, smoking moment–after she has been amused by his explanation of his injury but before she begins her tale–the narrator describes the woman, beginning with her scar and moving to her style. The passage highlights several aspects of the narrative at large:

> It was so grotesque a mark that one had the feeling it was the art of no human hand and could be peeled off like so much soiled putty. But this was a surgeon's office and the scar was real. It was as real as the honey-blond wig she wore, as real as her purple pantsuit. I studied her approvingly. Such women have a natural leaning toward the abstract expression of themselves. Their styles have private meanings, advertise secret distillations of their souls. Their figures, and their disfigurations, make meaningful statements. Subjectively, this woman was the true sister of the man who knows how to look while driving a purple Cadillac. Such craftsmen must be approached with subtlety if they are to be deciphered. "I've never seen a scar quite like that one," I began, glancing at my watch. Any minute Dr. Wayland would arrive and take off my bandages, removing me permanently from access to her sympathies. "Do you mind talking about what happened?" (99)

The idea that the narrator is approaching (or, perhaps, even possesses the ability to approach) the teller with "subtlety" here is, clearly, absurd. But his description does allow the narrator to make a "meaningful statement" about *himself* as much as one about the teller. For example, when the narrator writes about the "abstract expression" of the teller, he is revealing his own critical perspectives toward "such women." In the passage the narrator "reads" her as a cultural text, specifically using her bearing, attire, and size. He views her as an exotic primitive,[6] a distinct "type" of urban black woman. Above all, he reveals his own socio-cultural worldview with his description.

The above excerpt also reveals his investment in literacy. This passage simply could not exist in its present form without some previous acquisition of literacy, by either formal education, self-education, or some combination of the two. As such, it extends the literacy trope alluded to in the narrative's opening sentence. Jon Wallace argues that the narrator is

> Master . . . of what is primarily a white linguistic code [used] to look out at the world from deep within the safety of conventional institutions and ideologies that implicitly justify their failure to see beyond them. In their mouths Standard English becomes a defensive weapon–a means of self-protection that, like Standard English in the mouths of defensive Whites, enables them to "hold the floor" at the expense of speakers of other codes (language varieties or dialects) who want, and often desperately need, to be heard.[7]

This teller gives every indication of wanting, even desperately needing, to be heard. But her ability to improvise orally, as in her pointed response to his opening question above, balances their perspectives, regardless of his Standard English proficiency. Indeed, the woman does a fair amount of "reading" herself. Perhaps because of her previous experience with Billy Crawford, the narrator's mastery of literacy does not allow him to "hold the floor" at her expense. She is, after all, grounded in the African-American vernacular, and her response displays her own linguistic code, the one she uses to display her ability to "read" her world when the narrator asks her, again, about the scar:

> "I *knowed* you'd git back around to that," she answered, her brown eyes cruel and level with mine. "Black guys like you with them funny eyeglasses are a real trip. You got to know everything. You sit in corners and watch people." She brushed her face, then wiped her palm on the leg of her pantsuit. "I read you the minute you walk in here."
>
> "As your brother..." I began.
>
> "How can you be my brother when your mama's a man?" she said.
>
> We both laughed. (99)

She is, truly, "level" with him. She "reads" him in much the same way he "reads" her. Even though her critical perspective isn't based on literacy, her improvisatory employment of the dozens[8] effectively critiques his empty usage of the word "brother." Her description of the narrator as the type of African-American man who likes to "sit in corners and watch people" predicts her later description of Billy Crawford and the way he would sit "at a table against the wall, by hisself," talking disparagingly about those "good-timers and bullshitters 'cross the room" (100-01). If the narrator has successfully "typed" the teller, the teller has, equally as successfully, "typed" the narrator.

The words the narrator and the woman use are telling, as well. Not only is her smoke-blowing action "mean" and "deliberately irreverent and cold," not only are her brown eyes "cruel," but when Wallace calls the narrator's use of language "a defensive weapon–a means of self-protection," he uses the terminology of battle to describe the narrator's actions, as well. Ultimately, the battle terminology is appropriate, because the woman has barely begun her tale when the first of the narrator's two interruptions occurs.

The teller introduces the tale with "I was pretty once . . ." (99), and the background continues until she launches the plot: "I was twenty when it happen" (99). The teller then leisurely contextualizes "it," taking time to talk about the nature of the postal office, the place where the slashing occurred. She has just finished talking about how she rejected the sexual overtures of her white shift supervisor, and she's begun describing the "good people" who worked on her shift, "Leroy Boggs, Red Bone, 'Big Boy' Tyson, Freddy May...," when the narrator interrupts her "tiresome ramblings," as he puts it, and says, "What about that scar? . . . Which one of them cut you?" (100).

The narrator is not, obviously enough, the prototypically patient listener preferred by most storytellers. And his preoccupation with time, however understandable, doesn't help matters. Throughout the story, the narrator self-consciously glances at the office's glass door, expecting the doctor to arrive at any moment. As Wallace suggests, the narrator is interested in "discovering and imposing patterns on the world around him–patterns that suit *his* needs, *his* story about himself, and his relation to everyone else" (22).

He is, in other words, eminently worthy of her distrust. It is the very self-absorption Wallace identifies in the narrator that causes the woman to distrust him. He doesn't know how to listen. This first interruption, during which the narrator refers to the teller's long introduction and contextualization as "tiresome ramblings" (99), reveals the narrator's incompetency as a listener, quite possibly because he privileges literacy over orality. The woman reacts by reiterating her storytelling agency, pointedly demanding that he listen on her terms:

> Her face flashed a wall of brown fire. "This here's *my* story!" she muttered, eyeing me up and down with suspicion. "You dudes cain't stand to hear the whole of anything. You want everything broke down into little pieces." And she waved a knowing brown finger. "That's how come you got your nose all busted up. There's some things you have to take your time about." (100)

When the teller conflates the act of storytelling with the act of lovemaking, insisting that both are "things you have to take your time about," she also takes a firm pedagogical position. This teller is not only telling her tale, she is also explicitly attempting to develop the listener's competency, both "socially and morally" (Stepto 207). She is teaching him how to listen, particularly since his arrogant interruptions—in both form and fact—loudly suggest that he is incompetent.

But his reaction to her correction suggests that he is, at the very least, beginning to learn. After a section break, the narrator writes, "Again I glanced at my watch, but was careful to nod silent agreement with her wisdom" (100). This first interruption ends, then, with the narrator's implicit "agreement" to "take [his] time"—as best he can—and listen to the tale. The teller then resumes her tale, albeit warily: "'It was my boyfriend that caused it,' she continued in a slower, more cautious tone" (100).

Soon after the teller fends off the narrator's (first) interruption, she introduces the narrator's foil, Billy Crawford. Crawford not only dislikes the "dudes and girls from the back room" (101), he maintains that if "all them tried to be like him and advanced themselfs, the *Negro* wouldn't have no problems" (100, emphasis mine). The teller has previously used "Black guys" (99) and "black women" (100), as a broad identifying term for people of African descent; her attribution of the term "Negro" to Billy Crawford appears to be his own usage. Further, his attitudes about Negro advancement, along with his not being "ashamed," as the teller puts it, "to wear a white shirt and a black tie" (101) seem to fix him as a retrograde, boot-strap-pulling individualist. His determination to acquire literacy along with his explicit rejection of the "good-timers and bull-shitters 'cross the room" suggest a man apart, someone who feels he is "above" the rest of the post office blacks. "'Water seeks its own level, and people do, too,'" he tells the woman when they first meet, at lunch in the swing room. "'You are not one of the riffraff or else you would of sit with them . . .'" (100-01).

But literacy quickly becomes a contentious issue between Billy Crawford and the rest of the post office. Red Bone, a woman who aggressively controls the social life at the post office, shares with the teller why the rest of the black postal workers have started avoiding her:

> "She told me, 'People sayin you been wearing a high hat since you started goin' with the professor. The talk is you been throwin' around big words and developin' a strut just like his. Now I don't believe these reports, being your friend and sister, but I do think you oughta watch your step. I remember what my grandmama used to tell me: "It don't make no difference how well you fox-trot if everybody else is dancin' the two-step." . . . Use your mind, girl, and stop bein' silly. Everybody is watchin' you!'

> "I didn't say nothin', but what Red said started me to thinkin' harder than I had ever thought before." (103-4)

Red Bone designates the literacy/orality tension between the workers when she suggests that the teller had been altering her word usage to reflect Billy

Crawford's influence. It's impossible to tell whether or not Red Bone's charge is accurate, but Crawford's status as a man apart surely informs Red Bone's critique. Indeed, Red Bone's inclusion of her grandmother's saying crystallizes the tension between the individual and the collective at the post office, even as she reinforces her commitment to vernacular orality: the collective is to be valued above all, Red Bone insists; individuality "don't make no difference" if it brings you into conflict with the group.[9] Ironically, as Red Bone insists the teller is being shunned for "throwin' around big words"–an explicit anti-literacy, anti-intellectual swipe–in the next breath she urges, "*Use your mind*, girl . . . ." The teller then responds by "*thinkin'* harder than [she] had ever thought before"!

The teller does, indeed, begin to thoughtfully break Billy Crawford's behavior "down into little pieces": "I begin to watch Billy Crawford with a different kind of eye. I'd just turn around at certain times and catch him in his routines: readin', workin', eatin', runnin' his mouth about the same things all the time. Pretty soon I didn't have to watch him to know what he was doin'. He was more regular than Monday mornings" (104). She has successfully "read" his actions. This deconstruction and reconstruction of Billy Crawford's behavior leads the teller to decide that she needs someone more on her own "level"–the same term, ironically enough, Billy Crawford used when they first met.

Enter Teddy Johnson:

> "About this time a sweet-talkin' young dude was transferred to our branch from the 39th Street substation. The grapevine[10] said it was because he was makin' women-trouble over there and caused too many fights. I could see why. He dressed like he was settin' fashions every day; wore special-made bell-bottoms with so much flare they looked like they was starched. He wore two diamond rings on the little finger of his left hand that flashed while he was throwin' mail, and a gold tooth that sparkled all the time. His name was Teddy Johnson, but they called him 'Eldorado' because that was the kind of hog he drove. He was involved in numbers and other hustles and used the post office job for a front. He was a strong talker, a easy walker, that dude was a *woman* stalker! I have to give him credit. He was the last *true* son of the Great McDaddy–" (104-5)

The teller vividly introduces Teddy Johnson with such detailed and nuanced description that the narrator can likely visualize Johnson as a compelling and charismatic figure. Then she effortlessly segues into the language of a traditional black vernacular toast, using her verbal skill to liken Teddy Johnson to such black folkloric figures as Shine, Stag-o-lee or Dolomite.[11]

But just as her tale takes flight, the narrator interrupts her in mid-sentence:

> "Sister," I said quickly, overwhelmed suddenly by the burden of insight. "I *know* the man of whom you speak. There is no time for this gutter-patter and

indirection. Please, for my sake and for your own, avoid stuffing the shoes of the small with mythic homilies. This man was a bum, a hustler and a small-time punk. He broke up your romance with Billy, then he lived off you, cheated on you, cut you when you confronted him." So pathetic and gross seemed her elevation of the fellow that I abandoned all sense of caution. "Is your mind so *dead*," I continued, "did his switchblade slice so deep, do you have so little *respect* for yourself, or at least for the idea of *proportion* in this sad world, that you'd sit here and *praise* this brute!?" (105)

This passage recalls the predominant Tyler-Who Flung narrative in *Their Eyes Were Watching God*, where the porch-sitters, upon scant visual evidence, assume they know exactly what has happened to Janie when she returns to Eatonville, alone and wearing overalls.[12] In this instance, however, the narrator is referring to an extratextual narrative that stems from the very "crisis" McPherson's story critiques. As Patterson writes,

> Thomas Kochman found that . . . [t]he "mack man" who is good at "pimp talk" is a "person of considerable status in the street hierarchy." Two other students of the street culture, [Richard] Majors and [Janet Mancini] Billson, also report that, while Afro-American lower-class women may declare that they dislike the cool style, . . . "Black females are sometimes turned on by or attracted to Black males who act and look cool. Those males who do not act cool may suffer a heavy penalty of rejection. Some women are attracted to the urbane, emotionless, smooth, fearless, aloof, apparently masculine qualities of cool pose." (140)

In the narrator's mind, it is surely this "mack man," Teddy Johnson, who has seduced, abused, and then sliced the face of the teller. The narrator's interruption is intriguing not just for being incorrect, but for the assumptions and accusations he flings along the way. If (mistaken) gender assumptions such as this one are sustaining the "crisis" between African-American men and women, it is perhaps no surprise that the tension between the narrator and the teller is as palpable as it is. Perhaps most interesting is the possibility that the narrator has felt the "heavy penalty of rejection" Majors and Billson refer to above, since the teller repeatedly highlights similarities between the narrator and Billy Crawford–the latter of whom *did* slash the teller's face, and who *did* appear to be acting out of "rejection" when he did it.

The narrator's misreading, obviously based on the socio-cultural world view he exposed above, suggest two related possibilities: first, that he truly thinks the woman's mind is "dead." The narrator apparently assumes that the teller participates in the "double message" that some African-American women send to African-American men on the question of "cool." This narrator's misreading could very well be based on experience, but also could be associated with his literate education. (The scarred woman speculates that the narrator's intensely literal view of black culture is limited to "paper and movie plots" [106] rather than to lived experience.) Clearly, he is familiar with "cool pose," but he misreads its complex psychological position in African-American folklife.[13]

Secondly, his reaction appears to be based on the *form* of the teller's description. Perhaps this most skillfully rendered moment of the teller's tale leads the narrator to confuse storytelling craft for the mistakenly enthusiastic "elevation" of what he sees as a damaging, negative stereotype. In the absence of listening competence, the narrator, having "abandoned all sense of caution," hijacks her tale, attempting to bring it to a premature close by having it validate his assumptions. Part of his impulse is based on time. Insisting that "there is no time," he cuts across her tale, assuring her that he "knows" the Teddy Johnsons of the world. But apparently he knows them merely as men who have a "natural leaning toward the abstract expression of themselves," men whose "styles have private meanings, advertise secret distillations of their souls" (98-9). In other words, he only sees them as black exotica rather than as individuals.

When the narrator interrupted her, she was well into her tale, in the midst of the most important and emphatic sequence. The narrator writes, "She lit a second cigarette. Then dropping the match to the floor, she seemed to shudder, to struggle in contention with herself" (105). After establishing another time marker, the teller adopts a strategy of confrontation in order to make her point. Carefully using "a soft tone, much unlike her own," the teller momentarily stops her tale and "interviews" the narrator on his socio-cultural worldview. "You know everything," she announces as a preamble of sorts. "A black mama birthed you, let you suck her titty, cleaned your dirty drawers, and you still look at us through paper and movie plots" (105-6).

She begins the interview this way: "Would you believe me if I said that Teddy Johnson loved me, that this scar is to him what a weddin' ring is to another man? Would you believe that he was a better man than Billy?" (106). The narrator shakes his head in "firm disbelief," and the teller "seemed to smile to herself, although the scar, when she grimaced, made the expression more like a painful frown" (106). She then asks, "Then would you believe that I was the cause of Billy Crawford goin' crazy and not gettin' his college degree?" After his "nodded affirmation," the teller asked why. "'Because,' answers the narrator, '. . . from all I know already, that would seem to be the most likely consequence. I would expect the man to have been destroyed by the pressures placed on him. And, although you are my sister and a woman who has already suffered greatly, I must condemn you and your roughneck friends for this destruction of a man's ambitions'" (106).

The interview is revealing. His answers to the repeated phrase "Would you believe..." clearly mark the space where the narrator's assumptions rule his analysis. His "firm disbelief" confirms that space. The narrator, for his part, displays yet another familiar gender assumption: that black women routinely "destroy" black men by "the pressures" they place on them. While Patricia Hill Collins calls Michele Wallace's *Black Macho and the Myth of the Superwoman* "admittedly flawed" (9), Wallace's description of this "pressure" assumption is telling, particularly since her book was published within a year of McPherson's story:

> How did the black family respond to this pressure? . . . The Americanized black man's reaction to his inability to earn enough to support his family, his "impotence," his lack of concrete power, was to vent his resentment on the person in this society who could do least about it–his woman. His problem was that she was not a "woman." She, in turn, looked at the American ideal of manhood and took the only safe course her own fermenting rage and frustration could allow her. Her problem was that he was not a "man."[14]

The narrator, who steadfastly believes that the scarred woman is the cause of Billy Crawford's difficulties, is exhibiting a doctrinaire, seventies-era "Black Macho" perspective. "The Black woman had gotten out of hand," writes Wallace, offering an example of the way the reasoning went. "The black man never had a chance. . . . The black woman should be more submissive" (11). Curiously, the narrator doesn't refer to the love triangle as the specific source of Billy Crawford's problems. He highlights the "pressure" Crawford was under, and designates the teller as the cause of that pressure. Moreover, he aludes to the tension between the collective and the individual when he "condemns" the woman and her "roughneck friends" for "destroying" Crawford's ambitions. At no time does he suggest that Billy Crawford was responsible for his own actions.

The narrator attempts to be magnanimous as he acknowledges her sisterhood, womanhood, and suffering in his answer to her last question. But his assumptions reveal both the reason for her distrust of him and, ironically, the reason for his distrust of her–assuming that the above issues truly motivate his view of gender relations among African-American men and women. As in *Their Eyes Were Watching God*, there are competing narratives at work here. Even though Pheoby shared the porch-sitters' assumption of the Tyler-Who Flung narrative, she was an empathetic listener who was Janie's "kissin'-friend for twenty years" (7). This narrator has no personal relationship with the teller, and so his assumptions, based on his obvious cultural and experiential differences with the teller, make this storytelling session a fiercely contested one; the teller must marshal all of her storytelling acumen in order to attempt to overcome the distrust of her listener. In the process, she critiques their literacy differences, as well:

> "Now this is the way it happened," she fired at me, her eyes wide and rolling. "I want you to *write* it on whatever part of your brain that ain't already covered with page print. I want you to *remember* it every time you stare at a

scarred-up sister on the street, and *choke* on it before you can work up spit to
condemn her. I was *faithful* to that Billy Crawford. As faithful as a woman
could be to a man that don't ever let up or lean back and stop worryin' about
where he's gonna be ten years from last week. Life is to be *lived*, not traded
on like *dollars!* . . . But Billy couldn't see nothin' besides them *goddamn* books
in front of his face. . . . Whatever else Teddy Johnson was, he was a dude that
knowed how to live. He wasn't out to destroy life, you can believe *that!* (106)

The teller's previous reference to the "paper and movie plots"–a "reading" of
his "reading" of her story, by the way–is included in her scathing insistence
that he "*write* it on" his brain. The teller has effectively corrected the narrator's
misinterpretation of her story.

The narrator does not interrupt her again. The teller grimly recounts the
final confrontation: Red Bone, Teddy Johnson and the teller are sitting
together in the swing room when Billy Crawford arrives and insists the teller
leave with him. Although the tension among these four characters ostensibly
stems from Billy's command, the confrontation quickly takes the shape of a
discussion of the literacy-orality question. Red Bone signifies loudly, quickly
seizing the opportunity to drive the tense encounter to a climax that will prevent any subsequent confrontations, and her method seems to comment on
the literacy versus orality theme. She says to the teller, "You gonna let him
order you around like that?" The teller "didn't say nothin'." Red Bone then
turns to Teddy, and an extended riff on the word "say" begins, complete with
blues-like repetition:

"Red said to Teddy, 'Ain't you got something to say about this?' Teddy stood
up slow and swelled out his chest. He said, 'Yeah. I got somethin' to say,'
looking hard at Billy. But Billy just kept lookin' down at me. 'Let's go,' he said.
'What you got to say?' Red Bone said to Teddy. Teddy said to me, 'Why don't
you tell the dude, baby?' But I didn't say nothin'." (110)

This is an implicit nod to orality; it's a narrative gesture that suggests the
"swing room" inhabitants' sole investment in orality and anti-literacy is as
unwise as Billy Crawford's–and the narrator's–investment in literacy. Red
Bone subsequently says to Billy Crawford, "Why don't you go back to bed
with them *goddamn books, punk!* And leave decent folks *alone!*" Before long, the
teller has found her voice. She says, "I ain't goin' *nowhere!*" And as she tries to
"git to his face" he "slashes" her with the knife. The teller ends the tale with
"'some woman's voice that might have been mine screamin' over and over,
"You devil!...You *devil!*"'" (111).

"She lit a third cigarette" begins the close frame (111). The narrator writes
that "A terrifying fog of silence and sickness crept into the small room, and
there was no longer the smell of medicine" (111). The narrator ponders the
tale, his reaction demonstrated by a string of sentences and responses, such as,

"I dared not steal a glance at my watch, although by this time Dr. Wayland was agonizingly late" (111). The teller is subdued, as well. She says she just wants the doctor to "fix the part around [her] eye," adding, "People say the rest don't look too bad." The narrator "clutched a random magazine and did not answer. Nor did I look at her," he adds (112). He is, to be sure, the very same brash, presumptuous man he was before the tale–he does say, in the last paragraph, "I resolved to put aside all notions of civility and go into the office before her, as was my right" (112). But it is also clear that the tale has touched him in ways that he cannot ignore.

Perhaps it is not surprising that, for the narrator, the act of reading is now more than simply a welcome diversion; it is a coda to the tale's literacy/orality commentary. But the narrator isn't really "reading" the magazine, at any rate; his mind is obviously elsewhere. The story ends this way: "And then I remembered the most important question, without which the entire exchange would have been wasted. I turned to the woman, now drawn together in the red plastic chair, as if struggling to sleep in a cold bed. 'Sister,' I said, careful to maintain a casual air. 'Sister...what is your name?'"

Jon Wallace reads that last paragraph as a continuation of the story-long tension between the two patients. He sees the ending as a way for the narrator to "keep his distance by reducing intimate discourse to mere form" (24). Joseph T. Cox, on the other hand, suggests that the ending helps the short story "challenge preconceived assumptions" on the narrator's part:

> As the woman in the doctor's room explains the story of her scar, the narrator's flip curiosity turns to sympathy, and he remembers too late the most important question he should have asked: "What is your name?" He learns, as McPherson hopes his readers learn, to recognize himself in the deeper human dimension of the story and to feel some responsibility for someone who in the true sense of the word is his "sister."[15]

Similarly, Herman Beavers suggests that the narrator's ability to narrate the story at all–having turned, apparently, his waiting room listener-role into (written) storyteller–is evidence that "the scarred woman exert[ed] authorial control over her tale in order for the narrator to achieve a better understanding of women, which he then exhibits as a storyteller, having learned the art of listening."[16] Beavers sees the story as a way for the teller to help the narrator solve his assumptions about male-female relationships as well as assist his listening competency. The existence of the story itself, he implies, suggests that the narrator has successfully internalized each of the teller's underlying motives for telling the tale.

I'm not so certain this singular storytelling event can be so decisively effective. I believe the narrator's story-opening question about the teller's scar, and the woman's various answers, including the tale itself, have served as an elongated, multi-level *introduction*, signified by the anticipated ritual exchange of names. The narrator's urgent need to know her name signals his growing understanding that she is an individual. Her name makes her real; her bearing, attire and size may appear as signs that suggest she belongs to a collective, to a distinct African-American tradition, but she relates to that tradition as an individual. His wanting to know her name confirms his new-found knowledge of *who she is* by a need to know *what she's called*.

It is also a nod toward orality. It would take several lifetimes of stories–at least–to decisively resolve the literacy/orality question. Even if the narrator has achieved the competency Beavers argues he has, it appears that he still has a literacy-based way of looking at the world. Similarly, the scarred woman will still be an orality-based master storyteller who retains an analytical aspect to her personality. The difference is that this storytelling event has helped close the gap between the two poles. His "clutch[ing] at a random magazine" along with his insistence that the asking of her name is "the most important question" (112) roughly suggests a literacy-orality *equation*. Near the end of a story of repeated attempts to privilege literacy over orality and vice-versa, the story ends with a symbolic grudging acceptance of both.

Perhaps more than anything else, though, this storytelling event introduces the narrator to a less investment-oriented approach to storytelling. By the end of the story, the "narrative negotiations" between the narrator and the teller have come to a close. The woman's climactic statement–"Life is to be *lived*, not traded on like *dollars!*" (106)–is a qualified response to the narrator's initial investment strategy of offering his own statement in order to gain the best possible "returns" (97). She seems to argue that narrative negotiations are best executed implicitly, rather than explicitly. Certainly, storytelling is, as the narrator states, an "exchange" (112), a transaction, but her instruction suggests that perhaps storytelling works best when the participants don't have a too-conscious sense of *quid pro quo*. That same lesson applies to narrative negotiations attendant to the "tension" between African-American men and women.

Patterson does, after all, use present tense as he discusses the "crisis" of gender relations among African-Americans. He specifically mentions two other moments when black gender concerns attracted public debate: the filmed version of Alice Walker's *The Color Purple* in the 1980s, and, to a lesser extent, the publication of Terry McMillan's novel *Waiting To Exhale* in the mid-1990s. And the subtitle of Patterson's book–*Consequences of Slavery in Two American Centuries*–certainly suggests such longstanding problems will continue to be longstanding. But in "The Story of a Scar," as we will see in chapter five in Toni Cade Bambara's "My Man Bovanne," McPherson effectively constructs a narrative that employs a complex, multifaceted storytelling event—one that accomplishes, even with all the still-unresolved anger, distrust and suspicion, a form of dialogue that allows these two waiting room patients a way, at last, to connect.

CHAPTER 5

From Within the Frame
Narrative Negotiations with the Black Aesthetic in Toni Cade Bambara's "My Man Bovanne"

In *Invisible Man*, Ralph Ellison employs the blues as a way to approach "the absurd predicament in which Negroes find themselves upon the assumption that all is completely logical."[1] Jim Trueblood emerges as the bluesman-survivor, the transcendent personality who, as I argue above, ultimately acts, along with the vet, Brother Tarp, and others, as a model for Invisible Man—who eventually comes to a blues-like realization himself. But the blues, at its roots, is connected to the African-American agrarian experience. For example, Houston A. Baker, Jr., in *Blues, Ideology, and Afro-American Literature*, uses a rural railway junction as his central image of the blues, augmenting his analysis with a 1938 photo of three black men "sitting on the steps of the T&P Railway station" in New Roads, Louisiana, where, the caption reads, "One train per day passes."[2] Baker illustrates his blues matrix with rural imagery, including a singer who "draws into his repertoire hollers, cries, whoops, and moans of black men and women working in the fields without recompense. The performance," Baker continues, "can be cryptically conceived, therefore, in terms suggested by the bluesman Booker White, who said, 'The foundation of the blues is working behind a mule way back in slavery time'" (8). Ellison's blues-as-context works, in part, because Invisible Man's story begins in the South. The blues element moves North along with Invisible Man, and blues theory is, by novel's end, profitably applied to the Negro in America, rather than just in the rural South.

Unlike the blues, jazz came into its own in the urban North. In *When Harlem Was in Vogue*, David Levering Lewis writes, "Fletcher Henderson was New York jazz in the flesh, and New York jazz—however derivative, polished, and commercial–was soon to be the dominant school as far as the record-buying, radio-listening public was concerned."[3] Northern jazz is "polished" and "commercial" and city-bound in a way that Southern blues is bound to the fields. Within the context of the city–specifically, Harlem–"Henderson's Rainbow Orchestra symbolized, purely and simply, the debut of jazz as a product for national consumption. Until the end of the twenties, the national jazz sound was the swinging syncopation of Henderson's orchestra–with the Cotton Club orchestra of Duke Ellington (even smoother and 'whiter') a close second. The Savoy jam sessions broadcast over the radio, were to American popular music what Dearborn was to transportation" (173). To be sure, jazz grew out of southern blues, and the Great Migration greatly influenced the northern reception of jazz music.[4] ("Many of our patrons are originally from the South," says Lincoln Theatre owner Mrs. Marie Downs in *When Harlem Was in Vogue*, "and they relish the entertainment these folks bring, New York cultivated tastes being laid aside for a time" [33].) Nevertheless, while the blues is fundamentally rooted in the rural antebellum south, jazz is a modernist, urban music.

Indeed, if the blues is signified by field workers and the Ellisonian "little man hidden behind the stove" (490) at Tuskegee's Chehaw Station, jazz is signified by cosmopolitan institutions such as A'Lelia Walker's Dark Tower in Harlem. Toni Cade Bambara alludes to this south/north dialectic in her short story "My Man Bovanne" (1972). "I ain't never been souther than Brooklyn Battery and no more country than the window box on my fire escape," says Mama Hazel, the central character. "And just yesterday my kids tellin me to take them countrified rags off my head and be cool."[5] The line between "country" and "cool" is roughly analogous to the division between rural blues and urban jazz and speaks to the differing notions of identity among African-Americans in the urban north versus the rural south. The south/north, rural/urban, blues/jazz metaphor is helpful when viewing African-American storytelling texts of the 1960s and 70s.

In the century-plus between Frederick Douglass's "The Heroic Slave" (1853) and Paule Marshall's "Reena" (1962), most novels and short stories that included an African-American storyteller depicted that storyteller telling his or her tales to an explicit inside-the-text listener. As we have seen in Charles W. Chesnutt's *The Conjure Woman*, Zora Neale Hurston's *Their Eyes Were Watching God*, and Ellison's *Invisible Man* and James Alan McPherson's "The Story of a Scar," African-American storytelling was periodically "framed," often by a listener who was the text's narrator. But in the 1960s African-American culture was undergoing a profound shift on several fronts, all pushing outward against a framing status quo. The civil rights movement's attempt to end segregation was, at base, a struggle against a legal framework that restricted black freedom of movement. At the same time, the sixties-era revolution in jazz—called, variously, the New Thing, "avant-garde," or Free Jazz—was pushing against its post-bop frame, as well. The "head," the opening theme that frames the traditional improvised solo (solos that have been called "telling stories" by countless jazz musicians), was altered significantly and sometimes done away with altogether by artists such as Albert Ayler, Ornette Coleman, Archie Shepp and John Coltrane.

In the midst of the frame-smashing of the sixties, some African American writers staged their own rebellion by turning away from "protest" literature to speak directly to "the people." Like the civil rights movement and those radical jazz musicians, creative writers also staged a formal rebellion.[6] Black fiction writers who wrote stories that featured the convention of the black spoken voice allowed their fictive storytellers to speak without explicit inside-the-text listeners or third-person mediation in order to attempt to connect with "the people" as part of the Black Arts Movement.

Ultimately, Bambara's "My Man Bovanne" is an example of a "frameless storytelling event"—and I am well aware of the seeming contradiction in terms. After I reveal the contextual "frame(s)" around the story, including written African-American storytelling literary convention, the Black Aesthetic influence, and the corresponding difficulties of the sixties-era black feminists, I will then examine the story itself, using Gerard Prince's theory of the narrator/narratee to explain the relationship between Mama Hazel and her "listener(s)."

The connection between the increased number of black narratives that didn't use a narrative frame and the growth of the social movements of the sixties is an important one.[7] Hoyt W. Fuller contends, for example, that "white America has never been willing to listen to the authentic voice of black America." He then quotes black critic June Meyer, who says, "The definitely *preferred* form of communication, black to white, is *through* a white interme-diary. . ." (italics in text).[8] Although Raymond Hedin is speaking in a slightly different context, his conclusion is the same, apparently, as the sixties-era African-American writers: with such "severe restriction[s] on teller and tale," he suggests, "better perhaps to step outside the frame altogether."[9]

It was not until the 1960s that African-American writers did so *en masse*. "There is a revolution in black literature in America," writes Fuller in "The New Black Literature: Protest or Affirmation." "It is seeking new forms, new limits, new shapes. . . . The creators of the new black literature are deeply con-cerned with image and myth. They are about the business of destroying those images and myths that have crippled and degraded black people, and the insti-tution of new images and myths that will liberate them" (346). Indeed, Bambara seems to be referring to the idea of transcending frames when she says, "[W]e will have to invent . . . new forms, new modes and new idioms. I think we have to connect language in that kind of way. . . . It's become an obsession with me now. I'm trying to break words open and get at the bones, deal with symbols as though they were atoms. I'm trying to find out not only how a word gains its meaning, but how a word gains its power."[10]

Twentieth-century African-American literary history makes it clear that this search for "new forms" was futile; "frameless" storytelling events had appeared periodically throughout the century. But the search did spark more widespread use of "frameless" tales in African-American fiction. Although Bambara gave the above interview after *Gorilla, My Love* was published, her sentiments hint at the way her attempt to expand narrative form—by removing the frame—augmented her message, as did the formal explorations of her fellow sixties and seventies poets and writers.

Bambara's spoken-voice narrator in "My Man Bovanne" would likely have been framed earlier in the century. Although Hedin calls Sutton Griggs's narrator "the first free-standing, first-person black narrator in black fiction" (190) the voice is not a spoken voice. Nor is the first-person narration of James Weldon Johnson's *The Autobiography of an Ex-Coloured Man*, nor is Jean Toomer's *Cane*. It is difficult to pinpoint the first story or novel that featured a narrator who "talked" in an unframed story, and while not "new," this literary conceit clearly became quite common thirty years ago.[11]

Bambara's story was first published in *Black World* in 1971 under the name "Mama Hazel Takes To Her Bed" and was included in *Gorilla, My Love* under the current name the following year. Bambara's unframed story, intentionally or not, sends two related signals: first, sixties-era white readers need no instruction. The white audience is assumed to be competent—if they're reading the piece at all—and even if they are not, the black writer is not concerned with providing a model (Douglass's Listwell, Chestnut's John and Annie, Ellison's Mr. Norton, among others) for white readers to emulate. In a sense, the implied audience is the exact opposite of *Invisible Man*. Instead of writing to a white audience and assuming a black one, writers such as Bambara are writing *to* blacks and assuming a white audience. Additionally, unlike Hurston's *Their Eyes Were Watching God* or McPherson's "The Story of a Scar," the assumption here is that the black audience doesn't need a mediating frame, either. The implication is that the social context of the times is more than enough to allow a black audience to understand the "spoken" text. Certainly, the events of the story are rendered in such a way that the reader is expected to be able to identify with them. Bambara appears to apply readily the Hurstonian notion that "you got tuh *go* there tuh *know* there"[12] and assumes that most black readers have, indeed, gone there. The idea of an explicit listener to act as model is, then, superfluous.

But as Bambara and other African-American writers were busy attempting to make black literature "new," Black Aestheticians were just as busy attempting to define just exactly what the black aesthetic was. If there was a socio-cultural contextual frame surrounding the frameless narrative "My Man Bovanne," the socio-historical Black Aesthetic movement was a less abstract, far more vocal frame as well. Indeed, the Black Aesthetic movement went far beyond merely suggesting that black writers represent an authentic black reality to black audiences rather than white.[13] Black Aesthetic critics may have had a difficult time defining just exactly what the black aesthetic was, but they were, nevertheless, quite clear about the subject matter the black arts should have. Julian Mayfield's essay, "You Touch My Black Aesthetic and I'll Touch Yours" in *The Black Aesthetic* is a good example of the conundrum: "At the risk of sounding superstitious, I know deep down in my guts what [the Black Aesthetic] means, but so does every other writer who is grappling with this question, and some of them sound as silly to me as I must sound to them. This is not a cop-out, for like many another of our new terms, Black Aesthetic is easier to define in the negative. I know quite definitely what Black Esthetic [sic] is not."[14] Mayfield spends the rest of the essay defining it "in the negative," and comes to the conclusion that "For those of us who read and write books and plays and poetry, the Black Aesthetic has to do with both love and killing, and learning to live, and *survive*, in a nation of killers," that the Black Aesthetic, "for those trying to create today, is necessarily the business of making revolution, for we have tried everything else" (31). For the Black Aestheticians, Fuller maintains, "The black revolt is as palpable in letters as it is in the streets" (*The Black Aesthetic* 3).

Audience was an important part of that revolt. "The Black Arts Movement," writes Larry Neal in his essay of the same name, ". . . speaks directly to black people."[15] James T. Steward, similarly, stresses the importance of models in the Black Arts movement: "The dilemma of the 'Negro' artist is that he makes assumptions based on the wrong models. He makes assumptions based on white models. These assumptions are not only wrong, they are even antithetical to his existence. The black artist must construct models which correspond to his own reality. The models must be non-white. Our models must be consistent with a black style, our natural aesthetic styles, and our moral and spiritual styles."[16] "My Man Bovanne," largely set in a black political rally and focused on a black family, does "construct models" that correspond to a black reality. But Steward's insistent "must," his urgent demand that Bambara, and all black artists, create Black Aesthetic texts from a "reality" that the Black Aestheticians articulated, carried the Black Aesthetic impulse from a descriptive to a prescriptive mode. As we shall see, Bambara, as a result, constructs a counter-narrative that addresses the need for artistic freedom in addition to solidarity with the black revolution.

But Bambara's story also addresses the black women's role in the revolution, an issue so contentious that the Black Aestheticians reserved one entire *set* of "musts" for it. For a writer/activist such as Bambara, the rise of the women's movement quickly created a dilemma: which "ism" gets the primary emphasis–feminism or racism?[17]

Bambara's *The Black Woman* (1970), an anthology of black women's poetry, essays and short stories, was a substantive answer to that question. The collection was an important, early indication that African-American females were not to be marginalized–at least, not without a fight–in the Black Aesthetic debate. Bambara was intimately familiar with the difficulty of maintaining allegiance to the revolution and still struggling for equal rights as women (as were, surely, most women working in the Movement in those years). And just as Bambara edited her anthology as a "hardheaded attempt" for black men and women "to get basic with each other,"[18] short stories like "My Man Bovanne" also emerged as a means of reflecting "the preoccupations of the contemporary Black woman in this country" (11)–and, as such, another "frame" surrounding the story is revealed. Bambara's story echoes other literary texts of the era (primarily by black women writers) who interrogate the Black Power Movement, the Black Nationalist Movement, the Black Arts Movement, and the Black Aesthetic.

For example, "My Man Bovanne" recalls "Everyday Use," Alice Walker's fictional commentary on black essentialism, in a number of ways. The chief conflict in "Everyday Use" also stems from the relationship between a mother and a child who has joined the Movement. Dee (Wangero), like Hazel's children, demonstrates her newfound black consciousness by seeing everything that she used to disparage as a youth through new, revolutionary eyes. "I never knew how lovely these benches are,"[19] Dee (Wangero) exclaims. She covets her Grandma Dee's handmade churn and butter dish as well, holding them up as black artifacts, as literal signs of essential blackness.

But it is the old, hand-stitched quilts she admires more than anything else, and Dee's condescending tone echoes that of Hazel's children when she dismisses her sister's claim on the quilts. "'Maggie can't appreciate these quilts!' she said. 'She'd probably be backward enough to put them to everyday use'" (57). In response, Dee's mother, the narrator, thinks, "I didn't want to bring up how I had offered Dee (Wangero) a quilt when she went away to college. Then she had told me they were old-fashioned, out of style" (57). The urban/rural, "country"/"cool" tension is as evident in "Everyday Use" as it is in "My Man Bovanne." Both Bambara and Walker wrote stories in which middle-aged 1960s-era mothers attempt to keep their balance while standing on the shifting sands of black identity.

Both of these mothers demonstrate allegiance to the struggle, however. In an important aside, the narrator of "Everyday Use" talks about those "beef-cattle peoples" who said "'Asalamalakim' when they met you. . . . When the white folks poisoned some of the herd the men stayed up all night with rifles in their hands. I walked a mile and a half just to see the sight" (54). In much the same way Hazel supports the black revolution–her children's disruptive pressure notwithstanding–Walker's narrator also revels in a black show of strength. The bottom-line political stances of their central characters allow Bambara and Walker to walk the line between the struggle against sexism on the one hand and racism on the other–and still emerge as full-scale supporters of black revolution.[20]

Perhaps the most important difference between the two stories is Bambara's chosen voice for her first-person narrator. Walker's first-person story sounds written instead of spoken. Indeed, the narrator's voice, when she speaks in conversation, uses sentences such as this one, in response to Dee's claim that Maggie would actually "use" the quilts instead of hanging them: "'I reckon she would . . . God knows I been saving 'em for long enough with nobody using 'em'" (57). Walker uses "I been" for "I've been" and "'em" for "them" when the narrator speaks aloud to another character. But the Standard English narratorial voice allows the same character to describe Dee's teenage classmates with such sentences as, "Furtive boys in pink shirts hanging about on washday after school. Nervous girls who never laughed. Impressed with her, they worshipped the well-turned phrase, the cute shape, the scalding humor that erupted like bubbles in lye" (51). As Gayl Jones asserts, "Not until James Baldwin, Ernest Gaines, Ellease Southerland, Toni Cade Bambara, Ntozake Shange, to name but a few contemporary writers, did the folk language become flexible enough to enter the fabric of the narrative to tell the whole story."[21]

Indeed, today it is not at all uncommon to find first-person stories and novels that, like Bambara's Mama Hazel, sound very much as if they are being told to an active listener although there is no explicit listener in the text. But since there is obviously a tale being told, the question, in an Ongian sense,[22] is who's listening? There is, in such stories, what Gerald Prince calls a "narratee" to whom the narrator addresses herself. "[T]he narratee can be a listener . . . or a reader," contends Prince. "Obviously a text may not necessarily say whether the narratee is a reader or a listener. In such cases, it could be said that the narratee is a reader when the narration is written . . . and a listener when the narration is oral."[23]

The narratee plays a prominent role throughout "My Man Bovanne," with Mama Hazel speaking directly to him or her constantly. With the recognition of the narratee, the story becomes, in a sense, "framed" by a narratee who has, in part, "the function of mediation" to perform. But while Bambara's narratee is an important extratextual consideration, he or she should not be confused with the "virtual reader," defined by Jane Tompkins as "the kind of reader the author thinks [she] is writing for, whom [she] endows with certain qualities, capacities, and tastes."[24] The content of Bambara's story, a discussion of the cleft between Black Power organizers' agency and the lack of agency on the part of their constituents, indicates there are, indeed, "narrative negotiations" occurring with an extratextual virtual reader.

The distinction between the narratee and the virtual reader is important. As we have seen in previous chapters, traditional frame stories consist of a teller, a listener who is a character (often the narrator), and a reader who, the writer hopes, takes his or her cues from the reaction of the inside-the-text listener. But there's no guarantee the reader will identify with the listener, thereby allowing the hoped-for "audience readjustment" to take place. As Robert Stepto writes,

> In tale after tale, considerable artistic energy is brought to the task of persuading readers to constitute themselves as listeners, the key issue affecting that activity being whether the reader is to pursue such self-transformations in accord with or at variance with the model of the listener found within the narrative itself. In other words, the competent reader of framed tales always must decide just how much he or she will or can submit to the model of listening which almost always is the dominating meta-plot of the tale.[25]

The uncertainty as to whether the reader can be persuaded speaks to the difference between the narratee and the virtual reader. In a traditional frame tale the narratee *is* the "model" (that most important of Black Aesthetic considerations) and the virtual reader holds the intended response "in accord with or at variance with the model."

"My Man Bovanne," then, is at once a frameless narrative and a *virtual* frame tale. In other words, it is, literally, without a frame. But since Mama Hazel is obviously speaking to a listener–even if that listener does not actually appear in the text–Hazel is "framed" by a listener who is "virtually" present. Indeed, there are several different types of virtual listeners to whom "My Man Bovanne" could be directed beyond the surface reading. With the number of references to age, for example, the story could be seen as a negotiation with youthful ageism in an attempt to widen the social space for older blacks who "mean to do [their] part" (10) in the struggle as well. However, the virtual reader I will concentrate on here is a Black Aesthetician.[26] With this short story, Bambara writes a tale whose outside-the-text narratee exists as a model for Black Aesthetic critics in hopes that they will understand that artistic freedom for black cultural producers in general–and black female cultural producers in specific–should be a viable part of the Black Aesthetic.

The story has three sections: a contextualizing opening section, a lengthy kitchen conference, and a closing section. Hazel pointedly addresses her narratee with this opening sentence: "Blind people got a hummin jones if you notice" (3). With this beginning, Bambara instantly establishes a voice that sounds as if it is speaking to an active listener in much the same way formal frame stories speak to inside-the-text listeners. The sentence not only establishes the voice, but it immediately situates the speaker in relation to her listening audience. And audience relations, as we have seen, were important in the sixties and seventies since, as Baker writes, "spokesmen for the Black Arts felt that poems and novels could (and *should*) be designed to move audiences to revolutionary action" (*Blues* 84). As a result, the "you" in Bambara's first sentence accomplishes an immediate intimacy with a knowing black narratee, one that could easily "notice" said "hummin jones" if he or she had not already done so. Phrases such as, "it's like you in church again with fat-chest ladies and old gents gruntin a hum low in the throat to whatever the preacher be saying" (3), give the impression that Hazel is talking to someone who, she apparently assumes, has *been* in a black church, and perhaps will be again soon. It is a warm-yet-authoritative voice that casually addresses the narratee as if he or she is a familiar.

But it is just as obvious that the narratee does *not* live on the block. Hazel makes that clear by the way she introduces My Man Bovanne as an integral member of the community–so integral that if her listener did live on the block he or she would know Bovanne already. Hazel's language implies an immediate black cultural intimacy, especially given that the narratee is from beyond the local neighborhood. "He ain't my man mind you," Hazel continues, "just a nice ole gent from the block that we all know cause he fixes things and the kids like him. Or used to fore Black Power got hold their minds and mess em around till they can't be civil to ole folks" (3). It is possible that the "you" in the previous quotation is a generic "you," a reference to "anyone" as opposed to a specific listener. But even if the "you" is read that way, the use of it indicates that Mama Hazel is, indeed, talking to a listener. It is a decidedly *oral* gesture that cements the spoken-voice nature of the tale. By the middle of the second paragraph, Bambara has established her community setting, the narratee, and the chief thematic source of conflict in the story: Black Power.

The opening section also consists of the narrator's account of the act that causes the spontaneous family meeting: her "chest to chest" dancing with My Man Bovanne, who is blind. After the "hummin jones" description, Hazel says, "So that's how come I asked My Man Bovanne to dance" (3). She reveals soon after, though, that she is also upset with the way "this Black party somethin or other" is behaving toward Bovanne, who is a "[n]ice man": "Which is not why they invited him. Grass roots you see. Me and Sister Taylor and the woman who does heads at Mamies and the man from the barber shop, we all there on account of we grass roots," an assertion that speaks to the hypocrisy of the organizers who, according to Miss Hazel, are taking the older members of the community for granted. She finally says, "So everybody passin sayin My Man Bovanne. Big deal, keep steppin and don't even stop a minute to get the man a drink or . . . tell him what's goin on" (4). It is not, then, solely the hummin jones that drove Mama Hazel to ask Bovanne to dance. It is in reaction to the organizers and participants of the rally, the "people standin round up in each other face talkin bout this and that but got no use for this blind man" (4-5). Once she takes her purposely oppositional dance with Bovanne, her children react and she is, in short order, "hauled . . . into the kitchen" (5).

The kitchen scene, in fact, has all the components of a storytelling event, with central character Hazel and her three children, Task, Elo, and Joe Lee all in attendance. But unlike, for example, Janie Crawford sitting on Nanny's lap listening to Nanny's slave narrative, Hazel's children, the putative "listeners," do not sit and they certainly don't listen–they actively engage in a power struggle with Mama Hazel over her behavior at the rally.

Indeed, the kitchen confrontation between mother and children is metaphorically tied to the struggle between black artists of the sixties and the Black Aesthetic critics. The struggle manifests itself in the kitchen as an oral exchange between two parties. Mama Hazel's children attempt to "frame" her behavior in much the same way listeners/narrators of formal frame stories' confined black speech. There are several moments during the kitchen exchange that demonstrate the inverse power differential between parent and child. As she dances with Bovanne, her youngest son, Task, approaches her as if "he the third grade monitor and I'm cuttin' up on the line to the assembly" (5). In other words, he treats her like a child, or, at the least, as if he is in charge. Hazel also alludes to her children acting as if they are law enforcement officials: "Pullin me out the party and hustlin me into some stranger's kitchen in the back of a bar just like the damn police," and, not long after, "Them standin there in their pretty clothes with drinks in they hands and gangin up on me, and me in the third-degree chair and nary an olive to my name. Felt just like the police got hold to me" (6).

Structurally, the interrogation in the kitchen is framed by the open and close sections of the story. The children act as cultural monitors, as the "law" of the family. The competition for agency and control echoes familiar frame-tale struggles over voice and freedom of expression. This is not, however, a story-within-a-story as such; even though the "open" and "close" segments surround the kitchen scene, there is no formal storytelling event in the middle of the story. The story itself is, technically, unframed. Yet, even though "My Man Bovanne" is not a frame text, African-American frame-narrative negotiations continue–this time, as Neal insists, with a black audience instead of a white one.[27] Many black writers of the era began creative projects "with the premise that there is a well-defined Afro-American audience. An audience that must see itself and the world in terms of its own interests."[28] Or, as Bambara puts it,

> What characterizes the current movement of the 60's is a turning away from the larger society and a turning toward each other. Our art, protest, dialogue no longer spring from the impulse to entertain, or to indulge or enlighten the conscience of the enemy; white people, whiteness, or racism; men, maleness, chauvinism: America or imperialism . . . depending on your viewpoint and your terror. Our energies now seem to be invested in and are in turn derived from a determination to touch and to unify. What typifies the current spirit is an embrace, an embrace of the community and a hard-headed attempt to get basic with each other. (*The Black Woman* 7)

The focus on a black audience rather than a general one in the 1960s signaled an important shift in black fiction. But while these were neither the first nor last black writers in African-American literary history to write for a black readership, it would be a mistake to assume a homogenous, monolithic black audience. To the contrary, Mama Hazel, as she sits in a strange kitchen, under attack from her children, is engaged in a metaphorical negotiating session with Black Power advocates, Black Nationalists, and Black Aesthetic critics *on behalf of* blacks who may disagree with the politics these groups espouse, or may sympathize with the cause but wish to support it in their own way. Mama Hazel represents the African-American artist grappling with the reality of Black Aesthetic criticism. The difficulty of just "being" an artist is exhibited here, and Hazel's situation is further compounded by the fact that she doesn't just stand for the late-sixties and early-seventies African-American artist. She also stands for the *female* African-American artist who is, literally, "hauled . . . into the kitchen" (5) for violating her children's (read: critics) idea of correct public decorum (read: aesthetic stance).

Hazel's attempt to bargain with her children early in the kitchen conversation is reminiscent of the way some African-American writers of the era attempted to strike a delicate balance between the dictates of the Black Aesthetic and their own artistic impulses. Hazel's grudging independence, illustrated by her insistence on dancing with Bovanne, was an adherence to her own agenda, one that included taking care of old folks–in this case Bovanne–because of all they'd done for the community. As Bambara traced the response to Hazel's independence, she crisply critiqued the way Black Aestheticians attempted to define and control what acceptably "black" was.

For example, before her children begin criticizing her "chest to chest" dancing with Bovanne, Hazel opens these charged negotiations by attempting counter their objections. "'I was just talking on the drums,'" she explains to them. "I figured drums was my best defense," she adds, in an aside to the narratee. "They can get ready for drums what with all this heritage business. . . . So I stuck to the drum story. 'Just drummin that's all,'" (5) she says, returning to her children. Hazel's attempt to bargain with her children is reminiscent of the way some African-American writers of the era attempted to balance the Black Aesthetic position and their own artistic agenda.

Not surprisingly, Task's response is to employ the standard nationalist critical motive of the time: I'm only doing this for your own good. "Look here, Mama . . . We just tryin to pull your coat. You were makin a spectacle of yourself out there dancing like that," he says (5). The implication, of course, is that she doesn't know enough to decide for herself. But the further implication is that *they* know how to fill that obvious informational void–*they* know what's good for her.[29]

But Bambara then takes a narrative step that makes a reading of this story as a critique of the relationship between sixties black artists and Black Aestheticians seem fairly obvious: she has Task codify–as he "hold[s] up his hand and tick[s] off the offenses"–exactly what it is about Hazel's behavior that disturbs the children. One: Her dress is too short, especially since, two, she's supposed to organize the council of elders. Three: she drinks too much. "[H]e grab another finger for the loudness," Hazel says. "'And then there's the dancin,'" he continues (7). He also implies that she uses too much profanity as he begins to run out of fingers. This condemnation of Hazel's behavior in the story's specific context is an example of the sort of reaction the Black Aestheticians had towards artists such as Ralph Ellison and Robert Hayden in the sixties' black literary context.[30]

Mama Hazel's response to Task's finger-tip tally was simple and direct: "You know what you all can kiss" (7). But before the meeting in the kitchen ends, Task makes an important proposition: "What we need is a family conference so we can get all this stuff cleared up and laid out on the table. . . . How's tomorrow night, Joe Lee?" (8). Hazel's immediate reaction is to take a feminist reading of the situation: "While Joe Lee being self-important I'm wondering who's doin the cookin and how come nobody ax me if I'm free and do I get a corsage and things like that" (8). However, Hazel's children leave before her feminist stance can be articulated. Then My Man Bovanne enters the kitchen, beginning the closing section, and the Hazel-Bovanne connection that started the story ends it: As she leaves the rally with Bovanne, Hazel wants to describe the nationalist setting for him, in particular how "the people bout to hear how we all gettin screwed and gotta form our own party and everybody there listenin and lookin. But instead I just haul the man out of there, and Joe Lee and his wife look at me like I'm terrible, but they ain't said boo to the man yet" (9).

Although Hazel doesn't describe this scene to My Man Bovanne, she does, obviously, tell her narratee. As a result of this inclusion, this important paragraph demonstrates to the narratee–and, hopefully, the virtual reader–that the meeting with her children has critically altered her thinking on the nationalist question, but hasn't stopped her from executing her own agenda. She is still with Bovanne, and she still braves "terrible" looks, but she also displays nationalist pride. The mixture of the two, when related to the Black Aesthetic/artistic vision debate, is telling. Certainly, as Charles Johnson and Trey Ellis, among many others, have written, even artists who didn't adopt the standards of the Black Aesthetic were influenced by the movement.[31] In that sense, even when the Black Aesthetic critics "lost," they won. Like a stubborn pea under a mattress, the Black Aestheticians were at least a consideration for virtually every African-American cultural producer of the sixties and much of the seventies. When Bambara demonstrates a nationalist influence on Hazel without a total collapse to her children's wishes, she displays an example of one type of reaction to the Black Aesthetic, a reaction that fits into artistic responses of the era that ranged from adoption (Dudley Randall, Gwendolyn Brooks) to brief flirtation (John Edgar Wideman, Stanley Crouch, Ishmael Reed), to uneasy coexistence (Paule Marshall, Michael Harper, Bambara herself) to the outright refusal of artists such as Ellison and Hayden.

But even though Hazel has negotiated her own personal agreement with her critics regarding her behavior (in other words, she sees what they mean but she does what she wants), her reaction to the idea of a family conference is even more instructive. Her immediate "You know what you all can kiss" reaction is, of course, understandable. But she is very much in favor of a family conference, even if she is going to have to negotiate that terrain as well. As she and Bovanne leave the rally, he asks where they're going. She tells him, among other things, "[Y]ou comin with me to the supermarket so I can pick up tomorrow's dinner, which is going to be a grand thing proper and you invited" (9). Hazel's acceptance of the family conference–on her own terms–echoes a comment Bambara made in an *Essence* article titled "Black Woman/Black Man: Closer Together or Further Apart? ...Compared to What?" published a year after *Gorilla, My Love*:

> I feel positive. No matter how nasty and foul things may seem between [the black man and the black woman], I am convinced that we are serious about building a nation, committed to finding new ways to be with each other and

are trying to resolve the old power questions between men and women on all levels of our relationships. I hope that the static typifying many discussions and/or arguments (especially when groups of us sit down to deal with charges and counter-charges) are simply a necessary part of the unity-disunity-unity process that characterizes any group engaged in self-criticism.[32]

As Task put it earlier, a "family conference" can get everything "laid out on the table." Bambara points to the establishment of a place where the hard task of negotiation can be worked out, and she exhibits the sort of pragmatic optimism that could make such a meeting successful.

Perhaps this conciliatory ending is the ultimate negotiation. Bambara was an active member of the revolutionary movement. In her preface to *The Black Woman*, she writes, "We are involved in a struggle for liberation: liberation from the exploitive and dehumanizing system of racism, from the manipulative control of a corporate society; liberation from the constrictive norms of 'mainstream' culture, from the synthetic myths that encourage us to fashion ourselves rashly from without (reaction) rather than from within (creation)" (7). In "My Man Bovanne," Bambara created from within the frame, critiqued from within, and as a result found a way to demonstrate allegiance to the Movement at large and still give Black Aestheticians a critical look at themselves.

But while writers like Bambara successfully created narratives that agreed with Hedin's suggestion that it was better to "step outside the frame altogether" (198), the literal frame-text storytelling event was no longer widely used. Historically, many African-American writers used an explicit literary frame as a way to mediate the black spoken voice for largely white audiences. And just as Ong suggests that the literary frame of Chaucer and Boccaccio disappeared when the medieval audience became more comfortable with reading, sixties-era African-American writers' focus on a black audience made the rhetorical need for a frame unnecessary. As a result, there was no need to "contain" or "mediate" black voices in black fiction. The explosion of blackness at the time, the increased social unrest and increased cultural arts visibility, led to a readership that made the creation of an explicit frame a needless exercise. The closing section of "My Man Bovanne" is evidence that Bambara felt confident that her readership would be able to identify with Hazel, regardless of her orality—indeed, *because* of her voice, not in spite of it. The text asks the reader to take sides but only on the question of the children's controlling behavior. Their beliefs are not in question.

The ending of the story is instructive:

> [Y]ou gots to take care of the older folks. And let them know they still
> needed to run the mimeo machine and keep the spark plugs clean and fix the
> mailboxes for folks who might get the breakfast program goin, and the school

for the little kids and the campaign and all. Cause old folks is the nation. That what Nisi was sayin and I mean to do my part. (9-10)

Even though she fought to maintain her behavioral autonomy all the while she was in the kitchen with her children, Hazel ends her tale by offering her narratee a four-square endorsement of the Movement in which her children are involved. The "I mean to do my part" statement makes that clear and unequivocal. And yet, Hazel's response to Bovanne's imagining that she is "a very pretty woman" ("'I surely am,' I say just like the hussy my daughter always say I was") demonstrates her ability simultaneously to defy, inhabit, and mock her daughter's (and by extension, all her children's) confining behavioral stance. Her oral display of independence speaks to her ultimate dismissal of their attempts to control her. She participates in the Black Power organization for the same reason she agrees to prepare for the family conference–because she wants to. The narrative clearly communicates this complicated conclusion because the narratee is so obviously lead to identify with Hazel. The virtual reader is forced to take sides: Bambara makes an investment throughout the story in the virtual reader's allegiance, and the payoff comes when the reader sees Hazel as an independent, positive force for the community.

Ultimately, Bambara's "My Man Bovanne" does three things. It engages the Black Aestheticians, Black Power advocates, et al, opening a dialogue (especially since she published it in *Black World,* where they were certain to see it) that serves as a "family conference" of sorts. Secondly, the story addresses the difficulty of straddling the line between struggling for feminism and against racism simultaneously–and said struggle is exhibited in such an affirmative manner that, more than likely, it would buoy and support those African-American women who were attempting dual struggles as well. Perhaps most importantly, though, Bambara, along with other black writers of the period whose oral black voices emerged "from within the frame," "liberated" the written representation of African-American oral storytelling. With audience as their chief consideration, writers like Bambara made the unframed story as familiar as the frame tale once was. Bambara's "frameless" storytelling event did not signal the death of the formal frame story as an African-American literary conceit. Although one might wonder, with a growing black readership base, who would need a frame at this late date,[33] in my concluding chapter, John Edgar Wideman's contemporary frame tale provides some answers.

CHAPTER 6

"Would she have believed any of it?"
Interrogating the Storytelling Motive in
John Edgar Wideman's "Doc's Story"

Beyond their respective storytelling events, the unifying thread that ties
Charles Chesnutt's conjure tales, Zora Neale Hurston's *Their Eyes Were
Watching God*, Ralph Ellison's *Invisible Man*, James Alan McPherson's "The
Story of a Scar" and Toni Cade Bambara's "My Man Bovanne" together is
Robert Stepto's "discourse of distrust": the writer's confrontation with "the
requisite presence, and frequently active role, of the distrusting American
reader–thinly disguised as an unreliable story listener–in storytelling texts."[1]
This discourse is founded on the principle that readers of storytelling texts
must address the internal listener as a model for or against the reader. As
Stepto writes, "the key issue . . . is whether the reader is to pursue such self-
transformations in accord with or at variance with the model of the listener
found within the narrative itself" (204). Each of the writers of these fictions
has demonstrated, in one way or another, their acute awareness of this "key
issue" of listenership/readership. I have discussed Chesnutt's use of the frame
story convention to speak to both sympathetic and skeptical whites as well as
implied black readers, Hurston's audience critique–both inside and outside
the text–in the open and close frame of *Their Eyes Were Watching God*, Ellison's
grappling with the fear that his readership would inevitably peg his text as
mere "raving" or "buggy jiving" late in his novel, McPherson's exploration of
literacy and orality as potential models for his readers, and Bambara's use of
an interior black code to critique a black nationalist implied reader. Each
writer, in one way or another, interacts with his or her readership, and, with
the exception of Bambara, each used a "model" for the reader to access. And

yet, each writer, again excepting Bambara, expresses concern that his or her narrative will be misinterpreted in some manner.

On one level, then, John Edgar Wideman's "Doc's Story" is the most "basic" of frame tales. The story, much like Chesnutt's dialect stories, offers two models: a sympathetic listener and a skeptical (potential) listener. There is a lengthy open frame, a tale (Doc's story), and then a short close-frame conclusion. When the tale has been told, the reader has a choice as to which model he or she can, to use Stepto's term, "submit." The problem is this: only the sympathetic model actually hears the story. The skeptical potential listener doesn't hear the story—she is not even aware the story has been told. The chief irony rests in the fact that the sympathetic listener is, ultimately, skeptical as to whether the girlfriend "would have believed any of it."[2]

In fact, the story's plot doesn't allow the central character to consider telling his girlfriend Doc's story; he doesn't hear the tale until after they have broken up. As such, he can't prevent a breakup by telling her what he has not yet heard. And the narrator does say, outright:

> If [the central character had] known Doc's story he would have said: *There's still a chance. There's always a chance. I mean this guy, Doc. Christ. He was stone blind. But he got out on the court and played. Over there. Right over there. On that very court across the hollow from us. It happened. I've talked to people about it many times. If Doc could do that, then anything's possible. We're possible. . .*
>
> *If a blind man could play basketball, surely we. . .* (11, italics in text)

But the rest of the final paragraph complicates the above paragraph's seemingly unbridled optimism, revealing the central character's nagging skepticism:

> If he had known Doc's story, would it have saved them? He hears himself saying the words. The ball arches from Doc's fingertips, the miracle of it sinking. Would she have believed any of it?

This story-closing struggle between the central character's optimism and realistic skepticism hinges upon his bottom-line distrust of the girlfriend as a cultural "reader." As such, "Doc's Story" works well for a discussion of the discourse of distrust, especially since that distrust is rooted in Wideman's knowledge of and reference to Chesnutt's similar distrust of his readers a hundred years earlier. Wideman uses "Doc's Story" in several ways: to comment on the social act of storytelling as well as its various uses, to illustrate a form of "blindness" that connects the internal and external tales, to signify on Chesnutt's dialect tales, and as a way to explore and extend the discourse of distrust in African-American written storytelling.

Early on, Wideman sets in motion an examination of the discourse of distrust by discussing stories and storytelling. The first paragraph's second sentence makes it obvious that the woman the central character is thinking of is white, and it becomes equally obvious that he is thinking of her as a past lover (the second paragraph begins with, "She'd left him in May" [1]). So the early storytelling commentary stresses healing: "Hanging out, becoming a regular at the basketball court across the street in Regent Park was how he'd coped. No questions asked. Just the circle of stories. If you didn't want to miss anything good you came early and stayed late. He learned to wait, to be patient" (2). In the next paragraph, the narrator writes, "He collects the stories they tell. He needs a story now. The right one now to get him through this long winter because she's gone and won't leave him alone" (2).

The central character is using storytelling as therapy, as a means to comfort. This, perhaps, accounts for his practice of cataloging stories. He "collects" the stories, he has "favorites" (3). Certainly, the central character privileges Doc's story; he can cite exactly when the story appeared: "Its orbit was unpredictable. Twice in one week, then only once more last summer. He'd only heard Doc's story three times, but that was enough to establish Doc behind and between the words of all the other stories. In a strange way Doc presided over the court. You didn't need to mention him. He was just there. Regent Park stories began with Doc and ended with Doc and everything in between was preparation, proof the circle was unbroken" (3-4). The ranking and ordering of stories leads to the presentation of Doc's story as "the one [that] had bothered him most" (3), and it becomes, for the central character, the ur-text of the stories told at the basketball courts. As a result, Doc becomes a spiritual presence over the court. Of all the stories he'd heard, then, Doc's story was the one that was the most therapeutic.

But intertwined within the therapeutic aspects of storylistening is the emphasis on learning to be patient, to be a good listener. The implication is that the central character once was *im*patient and had to be socialized into being a good listener by the act of playing at and hanging around the basketball court. Wideman emphases this point by saying it twice, using the same language both times. The first mention above is augmented by a second mention a page-and-a-half later: "He learned to be patient, learned his favorites would be repeated. . ." (3). Importantly, the central character, as a model for the reader, is seen not only as a person maturing into a competent listener but a model who is acquiring that competence by listening in a specific cultural time and space. Wideman's "Doc's Story" is similar, in setting and theme, to a section in Wideman's *Philadelphia Fire* where Cudjoe, that novel's central character, has just finished playing a game of pickup basketball in Philadelphia. Although he has played in Clark Park instead of Regent Park, where "Doc's Story" is set, the cultural setting is the same:

> Mellow reggae thumps from the open door of a car. A light crowd of
> hangers-on in groups by the curb, against the chain-link fence, around a

bench on the court, huddled at another bench farther away where the hollow
drops off from the path. Riffs of reefer, wine, beer. You smell yourself if you've
been playing. Cudjoe's in the cluster of men lounging around the bench in the
middle of the court's open side. Night dries his skin. He feels darker, the color
of a deep, purple bruise. He won't be able to walk tomorrow. Mostly players
around the bench, men who've just finished the last game of the evening,
each one relaxing in his own funk, cooling out, talking the game, beginning
to turn it into stories. . . .[3]

Wideman writes the central character of "Doc's Story" into existence by
having him mature into a competent listener in this particular cultural space.
In this setting, "His favorite stories made him giggle and laugh and hug the
others, like they hugged him when a story got so good nobody's legs could
hold them up. Some stories got under his skin in peculiar ways. Some he liked
to hear because they made the one performing them do crazy stuff with his
voice and body. He learned to be patient, learned his favorites would be
repeated, get a turn just like he got a turn on the joints and wine bottles cir-
culating the edges of the court" (3). Clearly, Wideman is not merely describing
past storytelling events here but exhibiting the pleasure the central character
feels in *belonging* to an intimate and active storytelling audience, one that mirrors participatory black audiences in such African-American cultural spaces as
the black church and many black-performer-and-majority-black-audience
musical performances.

Moreover, as the narrator describes the central character gradually
"learning" to become more competent in his participation as an audience
member, he becomes a better listener. This particular "cultural immersion"
method of becoming a competent listener is one his girlfriend cannot attain
(few whites can, really, except for those who have an intimate connection and
involvement with black culture). As such, the acquisition of storytelling competency here is, in part, a specifically black cultural component of the play-
ground basketball court that is not readily available to most white listeners. Of
the storytelling events I have examined above, only Ellison's Trueblood
episode has a racially mixed audience, and the duality and difficulty Invisible
Man experiences as a part of that mixed audience points to the problematic
nature of including the performative aspect of storytelling with the acquisition
of competency in the midst of a racially and culturally diverse audience. As a
result, when Stepto writes, "The basic written tale is fundamentally a framed
tale in which either the framed or framing narrative depicts a black storyteller's
white listener socially and morally maturing into competency" (207), or, further, writes of the way "the framed-tale structure is manipulated so that the
novice teller may confirm in a fresh way that *telling grows out of listening*" (211,
italics in text), the cultural setting must be taken into consideration as to just
how far the white[4] listener has to travel in order to become a competent.

Obviously, the reader's position is a more difficult one, given that he or she must rely on his or her own imagination to construct the cultural context supplied by the writer. Even when the narrator has provided the reader with a detailed description of the audience's environment such as the one above, the reader still cannot immediately access real-world memories of the pleasure of such an experience if he or she has not been a part of such a participatory audience. This block to a culturally intimate audience makes it that much more difficult (although certainly not impossible) to become competent. And the central character's girlfriend appears just such a character. The outside-the-text readership might have as difficult a time as the girlfriend would identifying with the tale. If so, the traditional motive for the writing of basic storytelling events would, as I will discuss in more detail below, become a questionable one.

Of Wideman's two inside-the-text models, one is a participant in the storytelling event that goes beyond mere listening, and the other model is presented as a skeptical listener who is as cut off from the actual storytelling setting as many of the readers would be. Even under the best, most sympathetic circumstances, the girlfriend would have difficulty acquiring competency in the same way her (ex)boyfriend does. The narrator has, at this early stage of the text, begun a surface-level discussion of stories, the therapeutic purpose they can hold, and the importance cultural context has in that therapy. In contrast to the previously discussed storytelling events by Chesnutt, Hurston, Ellison, McPherson, and Bambara, Wideman is talking expressly *about* storytelling even as he is in the process of constructing a storytelling event. His use of third-person enables the narrator to outline closely and highlight key storytelling aspects of the story instead of merely contextualizing with the open frame, telling the tale, and then providing a close frame with which to conclude, in most cases, both inside- and outside-the-frame storylines. Wideman does all of that here, but he also develops the tradition by commenting on at least one purpose of the tradition (therapy) even as he is in the process of executing that tradition.

Near the end of the open frame, the narrator tells his readers about the central character's interest in Doc's story. Recall that this segment of the story interprets the actions of Doc and the storytellers who tell Doc's story, changing Doc from merely an interesting character to a spiritual, almost supernatural being, an archetypal presence. And it is the central character who gives Doc this status. In Wideman's fiction, due to his practice of not using quotation marks to designate a speaker, it is occasionally difficult to tell who is speaking, narrator or character. But in this instance, the commentary seems very much to come from the central character, for reasons that the story at large soon makes clear.

From a discussion of storytelling and its use as therapy, Wideman moves to setting. Like John and Annie's piazza in *The Conjure Woman*; the porch of Joe Starks's store along with Janie's back porch in *Their Eyes*; and Trueblood's front porch in *Invisible Man*, "Doc's stoop" is described as a place where the basketball players would share "ice water . . . in the shade of Doc's little front yard" (4). The communal exchange of "good feeling and good talk" (4) on Doc's stoop alludes to the familiar house-bound setting utilized in much of American storytelling. Here, however, Doc's stoop is described in explicitly racial terms. "Some of Doc's neighbors would give them dirty looks. Didn't like a whole bunch of loud, sweaty, half-naked niggers backed up in their nice street where Doc was the only colored on the block" (4). Contrary to other storytelling events, Doc's stoop operates as an explicit site of resistance in addition to a setting for a potential storytelling event.

The narrator takes this moment to place the story in an overarching national racial context, using the academy's racial stratification of the late sixties as touchstone:

> Doc had played at the University. Same one where Doc taught for a while. They say Doc used to laugh when white people asked him if he was in the Athletic Department. No reason for niggers to be at the University if they weren't playing ball or coaching ball. At least that's what white people thought, and since they thought that way, that's the way it was. Never more than a sprinkle of black faces in the white sea of the University. Doc used to laugh till the joke got old. People freedom-marching and freedom-dying, Doc said, but some dumb stuff never changed. (4)

This paragraph is not at all necessary to drive the plot, but it is important to build a context for the story. The narrator refers to the American white supremacist mentality, and uses Doc's reaction to the University's assumptions to heighten the story's civil rights movement setting.

After investing so much time describing the archetypal porch setting, Wideman displaces this traditional storytelling setting by placing the actual storytelling event on the sideline of the basketball courts at Regent Park. These courts have become a cultural site of urban *blackness* in a way that the rural, race-neutral front porch has not. Nelson George, in *Elevating the Game: Black Men and Basketball*, argues for a link between such black art forms as basketball, jazz, rap, and the sermon: "What links . . . basketball moves with rapping, sermonizing, and soloing is that they all manifest a particular–and shared–African-American aesthetic."[5] Similarly, Arthur Ashe, in *A Hard Road to Glory*, refers to a "distinctive black style" that "featured speed, uncommon jumping ability and innovative passing skills."[6] This postwar style of basketball, writes George, came into prominence "in the midst of the Great Migration, the be-bop revolution, and a new kind of building which began to dot urban landscapes: high-rise housing projects. Urban parks near project basketball courts became," as George puts it, "a spiritual home" for "this Black athletic aesthetic" (73).

The fabled Rucker tournament, played at a park adjacent to a housing project in Harlem, is an example of this black basketball aesthetic in action. Barry Beckham's description of the tournament sounds similar to Clark Park in *Philadelphia Fire*, as he writes that the atmosphere courtside at the tournament was "special" because the

> rhythmic . . . astonishing . . . expression of . . . natural ability loosened spontaneously, something that goes naturally with the dude under the tree who is practicing a bop and the little girl standing under the basket with a fried chicken wing dangling from her fingers and the poor kid wearing plaid wool pants in this August heat because, you know, his parents can't afford to buy him anything else, and the smiling dude with a gold tooth in the top of his mouth who tilts a paper-wrapped bottle to his lips and the colors of all the clothes and the energy and the feel and the sound of the voices. (*Elevating the Game* 75)

Of course, there are many different settings for storytelling events beyond the rural porch. For example, Madison Washington updates Listwell on his tale while sitting on line in a chain gang in Frederick Douglass's "The Heroic Slave" (although another, more familiar setting in that same story is in front of a roaring fire). Still, when Wideman gives the tale a contemporary, urban, race-specific setting, he is following the new mode of storytelling-on-the-spot that writers such as James Alan McPherson (a doctor's waiting room in "The Story of a Scar") or Reginald McKnight (a crowded Senegalese restaurant in "How I Met Idi in the Bassi Dakaru Restaurant") have exhibited. Although the campfire or cabin settings of much of the storytelling in *The Chaneysville Incident*, for example, recall more traditional storytelling settings, Wideman toys with storytelling convention by marrying the atmosphere of the site to the instruction of the listener such that the listener's growing competency is multifaceted; he learns and benefits from his setting almost as much as he does from the tale itself. Wideman's choice of setting brings a contemporary immediacy to the storytelling event. As Stepto argues, contemporary storytelling texts "confirm, in their storytelling *about* storytelling, that storytelling has developed its own store of artistic conventions. . . . When our contemporary writers employ these conventions, they acknowledge that a particular tradition in Afro-American writing exists, and, knowingly or not, they place themselves within it" (213).

Given the obvious twisting of convention by Wideman, the courtside narrator of Doc's story is unidentified other than by his black speech and obvious membership in the courtside fraternity; after a short paragraph, the tale begins: "Don't nobody know why Doc's eyes start to going bad. It just happen" (5). This voice continues without interruption for twenty-seven paragraphs of varying lengths. In essence, the last line of the tale encapsulates the overriding theme of Doc's triumph of will over adversity: "Doc is Doc, you know. Held his own. . ." (10). The inner tale concerns Doc's blindness, a blindness that symbolizes the cultural blindness of the central character's ex-girlfriend in the outer tale. Doc's reaction to his blindness is the critical difference between Doc and the girlfriend. Doc became "blind as wood" (6), as the teller puts it, but, still, he "always be hanging at the court. . . . Eyes in his ears. Know you by your walk. He could tell if you wearing new sneaks, tell you if your old ones is laced or not. Know you by your breath. The holes you make in the air when you jump" (6). Doc persists in his participation in the culture of the court, refusing to allow his lack of sight to move him.

Although Doc is the focus of the inner tale, the information the narrator gives the reader before the actual tale begins contextualizes Doc's blindness, especially since there are no references to Doc and blindness until the internal tale begins. Even before the tale reveals his blindness, we learn that Doc brings a stoic, tenacious attitude to adversity. The description of the black players' activity on Doc's stoop—along with the inclusion of the white neighbor's reaction—ends as follows: "They say Doc didn't care. He was just out there like everybody else having a good time" (4). Moreover, the next paragraph alludes to an *Invisible Man*-like progression in the space between Doc's laughter and the cessation of that laughter. He had come to realize, as Ellison writes for his own novel, "he can satisfy the gods only by rebelling against them."[7]

It is within this "stoic" context that the reader, as the tale begins, discovers Doc's gradual eyesight failure. First he comes on the court with "goggles on. Like Kareem" (5). Soon, however, he has completely lost his sight. But Doc didn't allow his blindness, as some might have, to keep him from being "out here every weekend, steady rapping with the fellows and doing his foul-shot thing between games" (6-7). Doc not only shot fouls, but he "practiced . . . at night when people sleeping. . . . Blacker than the rentman's heart but don't make no nevermind to Doc, he be steady shooting fouls" (6). The spiritual aspect of Doc's existence and his spiritual relation to the basketball players at the Regent Park courts are expressed here when the teller says of Doc, "Always be somebody out there to chase the ball and throw it back. But shit, man. When Doc into his rhythm, didn't need nobody chase the ball. . . . Spooky if you didn't know Doc or know about foul shooting and understand when you got your shit together don't matter if you blindfolded. You put the motherfucker up and you know it spozed to come running back just like a dog with a stick in his mouth" (6). Doc and his off-hours practicing emphasize the sense that Doc, as the narrator writes earlier, "presided over the court," that he was "just there" (3-4).

Doc's solitary foul shot practice not only highlights Doc's blindness, but it also, in contrast, speaks to the girlfriend's blindness. It would be "Spooky if you didn't know Doc or know about foul shooting" only to someone who was *unaware* of foul-shooting and the way its success or failure often depends on confidence, concentration, and the strict adherence of the shooter to his or her foul-line ritual. The above sentence, as spoken, immediately prompts an either/or identification with foul-shooting—you either understand or you don't, in much the same way the central character's girlfriend didn't connect with black culture through storytelling, even though she "listened intently" (10).

But Doc's reaction to his blindness and the spiritual space he inhabits is even more apparent when the teller talks of how much the other players wanted to be a part of Doc's foul-shooting. On the Sunday in question, when Doc and Billy Moon go to the foul line, "Fellas hanging under the basket for the rebound. . . . [W]hen the ball drop through the net you want to be the one grab it and throw it back to Billy. You want to be out there part of Doc shooting fouls just like you want to run when the running's good." And when he shoots, "ain't a sound in the whole Johnson. Seems like everybody's heart stops. Everybody's breath behind that ball pushing it and steadying it so it drops through clean as new money" (7). Doc's persistence in spite of his blindness, along with his foul-shooting, unifies the men on the court and provides a sense of uplift that turns an "ordinary" day of basketball into an extraordinary, transcendent experience. Doc's refusal to allow his blindness to unduly constrict his basketball playing—let alone his status as "one the fellas"—inspires others on the basketball court. He is a savior, of sorts, because by sacrificing his sight, he "saves" the other players by giving them an additional insight to the human condition.

However, on that particular Sunday, Doc missed the foul shot badly. As the teller says, "Might hit the backboard if everybody blew on it real hard" (8). Sky, "one them skinny, jumping-jack young boys got pogo sticks for legs, one them kids go up and don't come back down till they ready" (8), jumped up, grabbed the ball, and jammed it through the hoop. The crowd, a second earlier focused intently on Doc, turns their attention to Sky: "Blam. A monster dunk and everybody break out in Goddamn. Do it, Sky, and Did you see that nigger get up? People slapping five and all that mess" (8). Soon Doc, who "ain't cracked smile the first" (8), has a short, charged confrontation with Sky. According to the teller, "People start to feeling bad" because Sky, "just a young, light-in-the-ass kid," actually meant no harm (8). This moment, at a point in the story where the narrative has not yet departed from realism, temporarily grounds Doc as decidedly non-mythical. Just as African-American trickster figures sometimes "trick" members of their own community as well as the chief (oppositional) power figure in order to maintain their status as independent, autonomous beings, here Doc opposed the will of the court community.

Doc's ultimate reaction to Sky's "help," though, catapults the tale from merely extraordinary to legendary. Finally, "Doc says, Forget it, Sky. Just don't play with my shots anymore. And then Doc say, Who has next winners? . . . I want to run" (9). The inner tale ends shortly thereafter. The fact that the teller ends his tale without describing Doc's actual playing is, perhaps, not surprising. The teller speaks directly to his courtside audience for the first time at the end of the tale.

> Did Doc play? What kinda question is that? What you think I been talking about all this time, man? Course he played. Why the fuck he be asking for winners less he was gon play? Helluva run as I remember. Overtime and shit. Don't remember who won. Somebody did, sure nuff. Leroy had him a strong unit. You know how he is. And Doc? Doc ain't been out on the court for a while but Doc is Doc, you know. Held his own. . . (10)

In this moment, the teller distrusts his listeners, even in this setting and with this audience. There is a defensive tone to the teller's ending of the inner tale, a sense that the teller doesn't *want* to describe too closely the actual playing of the game so Doc's elevated memory will be protected. "Held his own. . .," as three-word summary of, commentary on, and description of the game itself insists that a detailed account of a newly-blind man who refused to stop "hanging out" and shot fouls between games is one thing, but Doc's actually playing the game is far better left to the listener's–and reader's–imagination.

The first sentence of the next paragraph begins the close frame: "If he had tried to tell her about Doc, would it have made any difference?" This close frame *denouement* of "Doc's Story" strongly echoes Chesnutt's dialect tales. Although Julius typically ends his tales in a more concrete fashion than the teller does here, Chesnutt's short stories, particularly in *The Conjure Woman*, usually don't "end" until John, the narrator, reveals, either in a roundabout way or directly, how the result of Julius's telling of the tale either works to his advantage or doesn't. Chesnutt's close frame's purpose, then, is to tie the internal tale to the external storyline in a way that will provide a conclusion to the short story as a whole. "Doc's Story"'s close frame does just that–for here is where Wideman comments directly on the discourse of distrust.[8]

As he signifies on Chesnutt for "Doc's Story," Wideman refers to Chesnutt's own entry into the discourse of distrust in *The Conjure Woman*, most notably in "The Conjurer's Revenge." In the open frame of that story, Julius, referring to the idea that a man could be turned into a mule and back again, says to John and Annie, "'I dunno ez hit's wuf w'ile ter tell you diss. . . . I doan ha'dly 'spec' fer you ter b'lieve it."⁹ The signal difference between Chesnutt's conjure stories and "Doc's Story," however, is that Julius still goes on to tell them the tale of Primus and his club-foot. He tells the tale even after John says to Julius, "'No . . . I don't think it is very likely that you could make us believe it," and after the usually sympathetic Annie adds "severely" that it is "ridiculous nonsense" (107).

He doesn't eagerly volunteer the story, however. John narrates, "This reception of the old man's statement reduced him to silence, and it required some diplomacy on my part to induce him to vouchsafe an explanation. The prospect of a long, dull afternoon was not alluring, and I was glad to have the monotony of Sabbath quiet relieved by a plantation legend" (108). John adds, a sentence later, that Julius told his tale only "when I had finally prevailed upon him to tell us the story" (108). So even though Julius did go on to tell the tale, it is clear that his distrust of them had to be placated, at best–or, at worst, deferred–before he told the story. But he did, at last, tell it. Now, the frame-tale format of Chesnutt's conjure stories must be taken into account here. As we have seen, in almost every tale the open frame is in John's first person, and John regains control of the narrative in the close frame. In between, Julius tells his tale. So for practical reasons Julius *would* tell the tale of "The Conjurer's Revenge," his distrust of his listeners notwithstanding.

Wideman, unlike Chesnutt, allows his readers access to a story that the potential inside-the-text listener never hears. He lets his central character listen to the story at courtside and then shows him trying to decide whether it would have made any difference if he had told Doc's story to his former girl-friend. Thus he echoes Chesnutt's distrust of John and Annie by showing the central character wrestling with his distrust of his ex-girlfriend:

> If he had tried to tell her about Doc, would it have made a difference? Would the idea of a blind man playing basketball get her attention or would she have listened the way she listened when he told her stories he'd read about slavery days when Africans could fly, change themselves to cats and hummingbirds, when black hoodoo priests and conjure queens were feared by powerful whites even though ordinary black lives weren't worth a penny. To her it was folklore, superstition. Interesting because it revealed the psychology of the oppressed. She listened intently, not because she thought she'd hear the truth. For her, belief in magic was like belief in God. Nice work if you could get it. Her skepticism, her hardheaded practicality, like the smallness of her hands, appealed to him. Opposites attracting. But more and more as the years went by, he'd wanted her with him, wanted them to be together. . . (10)

Wideman explicitly ties his central character's contemporary distrust to Chesnutt's *The Conjure Woman* here, as the "stories" the central character has told his girlfriend correspond to tales of Dan turning Mahaly into "a black cat" (184) in "The Grey Wolf's Ha'nt" and Aunt Peggy turning "little Mose ter a hummin-bird" (147) in "Sis' Becky's Pickaninny." This direct reference to

Chesnutt, especially when he talks of "hoodoo priests and conjure queens" shortly thereafter, lends the possibility that "when he told her stories he'd read about slavery days," Chesnutt's *The Conjure Woman* was included.

Wideman, however, fuses John and Annie, representative of the analytical male and the compassionate female, into the central character's girlfriend, a singular, white *female* skeptic who represents, for Wideman, an updated exploration of the cultural differences in the 1980s, nearly one hundred years after Chesnutt's collection of stories. In "Doc's Story," Wideman uses a white woman dating a black man as a way to dissect the cultural differences between whites and blacks, differences that are present and divisive even when both parties urgently wish to bridge the gap. He speaks to the idea of "Opposites attracting," even though "more and more as the years went by, he'd wanted her with him, wanted them to be together. . ." (10). It is her "skepticism, her hardheaded practicality" (10) that he admires but that also helped keep them apart.

In the close frame, Wideman sets up this cultural opposition between the central character and the girlfriend–belief and nonbelief–and then places the tale in between them, allowing the tale to be "read" in markedly different ways. The central character reads Doc's stoic refusal to succumb to truly being "blind" as a blues moment, an example of what Ralph Ellison calls the "Negro American folk tradition" in "Change the Joke and Slip the Yoke"–a folkloric cultural force that has "much to tell us of the faith, humor, and adaptability to reality necessary to live in a world which has taken on much of the insecurity and blues-like absurdity known to those who brought it into being" (112). George Kent, quoted in *Speaking For You: The Vision of Ralph Ellison*, adds,

> Offering the first drawings of a group's character, preserving situations repeated in the history of the group, describing the boundaries of thought and feeling, projecting the group's wisdom in symbols expressing its will to survive, embodying those values by which it lives and dies, folklore seemed, as Ellison described it, basic to the portrayal of the essential spirit of black people.[10]

In short, the central character was enthralled not only with Doc's story but with the idea of storytelling as a survival strategy used by Africans-in-the-New World since they first arrived on these shores in 1619. The problem, for him, was the reaction he was (not) getting from his girlfriend. She would listen to the stories but would not (could not?) *believe* them.

The white girlfriend's starkly analytical view of the central character's stories as a window into the "pathology of the oppressed" is described in Lawrence Levine's *Black Culture and Black Consciousness* as "the popular formula which has rendered black history an unending round of degradation and pathology."[11] The central character's girlfriend expressed, in Levine's words, a "desire to see in the oppressed only unrelieved suffering and impotence" and held a belief in "the pure victim" instead of, through the use of folklore in its many forms, "black men and women [who] were able to find the means to sustain a far greater degree of self-pride and group cohesion than the system they lived under ever intended for them to be able to do" (xi).

The text of Doc's story, then, can be read in radically different ways based on who is listening–the central character or the girlfriend. The difference with Wideman's story is that he presents the central character's post-tale reading along side his ambivalence regarding whether his girlfriend "would have believed any of it" (11). Chesnutt, in his conjure stories, presented an *actual* dual post-tale reading of the tale in question, with, tellingly, John and Annie disagreeing more often than not. As I stated at the outset, however, it is Wideman's construction of the sequence of events that is crucial. Having the central character try to decide whether telling her *would have* made any difference is in stark contrast to the central character trying to decide whether *to* tell her. He says, declaratively, "If he'd known Doc's story he would have" told her about him. And even though he says, "*If Doc could do that, then anything's possible. We're possible. . .,*" two things are clear: first, the central character undercuts that certainty moments later when he asks, "If he had known Doc's story, would it have saved them?" in the story's last paragraph (11). Second, the question is, finally, moot. She's already left him. In that sense, the reader is left with the finality of her not having access to the story–even though there is at least some question in the central character's mind as to whether she would have believed it at all.

A hundred years has passed since the publishing of Chesnutt's "The Conjurer's Revenge." Julius's concern about his audience's "belief" comes at the beginning of the story and is, essentially, cast aside as the tale is told. Written during what Rayford Logan has called the "nadir"[12] (52) of the Negro existence in America, "The Conjurer's Revenge" is, nevertheless, hopeful. Even though John and Annie express their skepticism, Julius sets aside his distrust of them to tell the tale. Wideman's discussion of distrust, which comes near the end of "Doc's Story" and happens completely outside of the earshot of the central character's ex-girlfriend, is much less optimistic. Instead of posing the question and then going on to tell the tale, the story ends on a decidedly uncertain note: "If he had tried to tell her about Doc, would it have made a difference?" (10).

This is in marked contrast to the texts studied in my earlier chapters. Even when Janie submits that she's unsure whether the retelling of her story will alter the porch-sitters in any way, she doesn't mind the retelling since Pheoby obviously is quite sure it should–and would–influence them. And although Ellison's narrator is quite ambivalent about the "why" of his text in *Invisible*

Man's final pages, in accordance with the blues aesthetic he writes it "nonetheless"–to say nothing of the way Trueblood overcomes his distrust of Mr. Buchanan, Sheriff Barbour, and the rest of his initial white listeners.[13] McPherson's ending, as ambiguous as it is, can still be read as an incompetent listener beginning to "get it." And Bambara's tale, frameless as it is, builds on Ellison's guarded optimism with an unguardedly optimistic text.

"Doc's Story"'s central character's story-ending question also recalls similar quandaries in novels or short stories that contain storytelling events. John Washington, in David Bradley's *The Chaneysville Incident*, postpones his telling of the story of his ancestors not just because of the difficulty of reconciling historical "fact" with imagined "fiction," but because he distrusts his white girlfriend Judith's competence as a listener. Ernest Gaines's Miss Jane Pittman is also initially suspicious of the historian who comes to hear her life's story. The teller's distrust is palpable in each of these storytelling texts. And yet, in each case, the story is told. For the purposes of this discussion, it is far less important that "Doc's Story" is a Type B' tale[14] than is the fact that, doubts notwithstanding, *Their Eyes*'s Janie does ultimately allow her story to be told. Likewise, Miss Jane Pittman finally agrees to tell her story to the historian, and John Washington, in the end, tells his tale to Judith as well. As Stepto contends, the distrustful storyteller "first forges, then wields, then at strategic moments forsakes *his or her* distrust. . ." (212 italics in text).

In effect, though, "Doc's Story" interrogates the idea of the inside-the-text listener as model for outside-the-text reader. The sequence of events (i.e. their breakup) ultimately removes the ex-girlfriend's "potential" from her status as a potential listener. As a result of that displacement, along with the critical lack of resolution at story's end, Wideman fundamentally questions whether Chesnutt, or any of the rest of the storytelling events in African-American fiction, for that matter, actually do what they set out to do: change (white) American attitudes towards African-Americans or, in the case of Hurston and Bambara, change ways of thinking and being within the black community. If, indeed, the ex-girlfriend is the central character's opposing model, then her absence signals, finally, the text's unresolved distrust of the reader. The last sentence, "Would she have believed any of it?" (11), could, then, be a question for the skeptical reader of African-American storytelling writ large as well as the ex-girlfriend of this particular story: *Do you believe any of it?*

It is Wideman's authorial intervention, the purposeful arranging of the sequence of events in the story, and the questions that the *non*telling of the tale produces that gives the story its ultimate message: that the contemporary (white) reader, like the girlfriend inside the text, is still suspect, still worthy of distrust. In much the same way W.E.B. DuBois's famous "color line" declaration "framed" the present millennium, the ultimate question on which the story ends, "Would she have believed any of it?," remains the central question of African American written storytelling at the dawn of the twenty-first century.

Notes

NOTES TO THE INTRODUCTION

1. Geneviéve Fabre and Robert G. O'Meally, *History and Memory in African-American Culture* (New York: Oxford University Press, 1994), 4. All subsequent quotations are cited parenthetically in the text.

2. As John H. Pearson writes in "The Politics of Framing in the Late Nineteenth Century," "The frame's purpose . . . is to announce the closed, tectonic border that is presumed to exist between the conceptual realm of art, which it contains, and the world, in which it suggests the function of art as commodity. Therefore, these frames demark, as do all property lines (and city walls), a recognizable, verifiable difference between art and the world–a difference which, without the frame, would still somehow distinguish the two realms, though would not ensure the freedom of either realm from intrusion of the other" (17). In other words, the *difference* between what is inside and outside the frame–the text and the reader–remains with the absence of a frame; whoever includes a frame, however, "marks" that difference and controls the perception of that difference.

3. For more information about the African-American vernacular tradition, see "The Vernacular Tradition" (1-127) in *The Norton Anthology to African American Literature*, edited by Henry Louis Gates, Jr, et al.

4. There is no uniform sense of the difference between a frame text and an embedded narrative, however. In *Story and Situation: Narrative Seduction and the Power of Fiction* (Minneapolis: University of Minnesota Press, 1984), for instance, Ross Chambers refers to stories inside frame texts as embedded narratives the same way he does tales in larger works that are not strict frame texts. For the purposes of this study, I will continue to make the distinction between frame texts and embedded narratives as I have thus far in the introduction.

5. James Weldon Johnson, *The Autobiography of an Ex-Coloured Man* (New York: Vintage Books, 1989), 3.

6. Ralph Ellison, *Invisible Man* (New York: Vintage Books, 1989), 579.

7. Gloria Naylor, *Mama Day* (New York: Ticknor & Fields, 1988), 17.

8. Henry Louis Gates, Jr. and Nellie Y. McKay,eds, *The Norton Anthology of Afircan-American Literature* (New York: W. W. Norton, 1997), 2373.

9. Geneva Smitherman, *Talkin' and Testifyin': The Language of Black America* (Boston: Houghton Mifflin Company, 1977), 2. All subsequent quotations are cited parenthetically in the text.

10. Reginald McKnight, *Moustapha's Eclipse* (New York: Ecco Press, 1989), 5. All subsequent quotations are cited parenthetically in the text.

11. Perhaps the following quotation from *Blues People* (New York: William Morrow & Company, 1983), by Amiri Baraka (then LeRoi Jones) most effectively speaks to the possibilities of a broad interpretation of the African-American spoken voice:

> It is absurd to assume, as has been the tendency, among a great many Western anthropologists and sociologists, that all traces of Africa were erased from the Negro's mind because he learned English. The very nature of the English the Negro spoke and still speaks drops the lie on that idea. (9)

12. Robert Stepto, *From Behind the Veil: A Study of Afro-American Narrative,* 2nd edition (Urbana, Ill: University of Illinois Press, 1991), 33. All subsequent quotations are cited parenthetically in the text.

13. Gayl Jones, *Liberating Voices: Oral Tradition in African-American Literature* (Cambridge: Harvard University Press, 1991), 100.

14. John Edgar Wideman, "Frame and Dialect: The Evolution of the Black Voice," *The American Poetry Review* (Sept-Oct 1976), 33. All subsequent quotations are cited parenthetically in the text.

15. Walter Ong, S.J. *Interfaces of the Word: Studies in the Evolution of Consciousness and Culture* (Ithaca, NY: Cornel University Press, 1977), 59. All subsequent quotations are cited parenthetically in the text.

16. Below are a variety of significant frame stories throughout African-American literary history. Some are formal "frame" tales, some are "frameless," spoken-voice narratives, all deal in some way with a teller and a listener, real or implied: Victor Sejour, "The Mulatto" (1837); Frederick Douglass, "The Heroic Slave," (1852); Charles Waddell Chesnutt, *The Conjure Woman* (1899)[see chapter one]; Pauline Hopkins, "The Mystery Within Us," *Colored American Magazine* (1900); Paul Laurence Dunbar, *The Strength of Gideon* (1900); Zora Neale Hurston, "Magnolia Flower" (1925); Richard Nathaniel Wright, "Superstition," *Abbott's Monthly* (1931); Langston Hughes, "Passing" (1933) and "A Good Job Gone" (1933), *The Ways of White Folks* (1933); Ralph Ellison, "Hymie's Bull" (1937); Hurston, *Their Eyes Were Watching God* (1937)[see chapter two]; Ellison, "Flying Home" (1944), *Invisible Man* (1952)[see chapter three]; Paule Marshall, "Reena" (1961); Sherley Anne Williams, "Tell Martha Not to Moan" (1967); Ernest J. Gaines, *Of Love and Dust* (1967), "A Long Day in November" (1968), "The Sky is Gray" (1968); James Alan McPherson, "The Story of a Scar" (1970) [see chapter four],"A Solo Song: For Doc" (1970); Toni Cade Bambara, "Gorilla, My Love" (1971), "My Man Bovanne" (1971) [see chapter five]; Gaines, *Autobiography of Miss Jane Pittman* (1971); David Bradley, *The Chaneysville Incident* (1981); Rita Dove, "The Vibraphone," (1985); John Edgar Wideman, "Doc's Story" (1986) [see chapter six]; Reginald McKnight, *Moustapha's Eclipse* (1988), Wanda Coleman, "Lonnie's Cousin"

(1988); Terry McMillan, "Ma' Dear" (1987); McKnight, "Into Night," *The Kind of Light that Shines on Texas* (1992); Sapphire, *Push* (1996); McKnight, "The More I Like Flies" (1998); *He Sleeps* (2001).

17. Both of these stories can be found in *Breaking Ice: An Anthology of Contemporary African-American Fiction*, edited by Terry McMillan (New York: Penguin Books, 1990).

NOTES TO CHAPTER 1

1. James Weldon Johnson, "The Dilemma of the Negro Author," (*American Mercury* 15 (Dec 1928), 477. All subsequent quotations are cited parenthetically in the text.

2. It is instructive that the language Johnson uses in the above passage echoes two important assertions by W. E. B. DuBois. When Johnson says, the "Aframerican author faces a problem . . . the problem of the double audience," he is signifyin(g) on both DuBois's contention that the "problem of the Twentieth Century is the problem of the color line" (xiii) as well as DuBois's famous comment on the "double-consciousness" of African-Americans (3), both from *The Souls of Black Folk*.

3. Helen M. Chesnutt, *Charles Waddell Chesnutt: Pioneer of the Color Line* (Chapel Hill: University of North Carolina Press, 1952), 68. All subsequent quotations are cited parenthetically in the text.

4. Richard Baldwin sums it up this way: "The central problem was the audience. The reading public was predominantly white, and the audience that most early black writers cared most to reach was white, for it was to whites that they needed to tell the truth about the black experience in America" (385). Bone agrees: "Through the medium of fiction, Chesnutt proposes to create a moral revolution, by enlarging the white man's sympathies and sharpening his moral vision" (83). Robert Hemenway adds, "In terms of literary history, perhaps this method of addressing two audiences simultaneously was the only way a black writer could affirm the psychological resources of his people at a time when white supremacy had just regained control of the South, and the minstrel show was a major form of American entertainment" (302). And William Gleason suggests, finally, that Chesnutt took an archetectual approach, "that the meticulously framed conjure tales offered Chesnutt a surprisingly versatile form through which to elaborate a penetrating investigation into race, memory, and the built environment that, it turns out, he had been developing since his first published story" (34-5).

5. Characters like Uncle Remus or "Sam" in Thomas Nelson Page's "Marse Chan" ignored (or worse, grossly idealized and misrepresented) the reality of enslaved blacks day-to-day lives. Chesnutt's Uncle Julius "undercut the effect such fiction was having as proslavery, white supremacist propaganda," writes Lucinda MacKethan in *The History of Southern Literature*. "[T]he stories he tells to divert his white patrons contain portraits of masters in whom greed is the sole motivation and slaves for whom plantation life means separation from loved ones, hard labor, and sudden reversals at the whim of the masters" (216-17).

6. In *The Folk of Southern Fiction*, Merrill Maguire Skaggs dates "the tradition of the Old Southern Plantation where all was grace, sweetness, culture and light" (6) from 1832, the year John Pendleton Kennedy's *Swallow Barn* was first published. But she

insists it is the work of Thomas Nelson Page which "came to seem synonymous with southern romance": "'Marse Chan,'" she writes, "illustrates the Page formula and epitomizes the plantation legend as it appeared in fiction" (10). She adds, "One must always remember that the southern local colorist was extremely eager to represent his region in the best possible light. He had three widely recognized, accepted stereotypes to work with: the colorful plantation owner with his variously appealing family, the contented darky, and the contemptible poor white" (21).

7. David Britt claims that the *Conjure Woman* stories "are deliberately structured to allow the reader to be deceived about the more significant levels of meaning if he chooses, or needs, to be deceived" (271), and the book seems to have been received in just such a wide-ranging manner. Many reviewers did understand that while "none of [the stories] lacks those quiet touches of humor which are so characteristic of the negro character; . . . they are also full of side-lights on the tragedy of slave life–a tragedy which is brought into more striking relief because it comes out, so to speak, incidentally and by the way" (*The Outlook* [Feb. 24, 1900]: 441). However, letters to Chesnutt at the time do not mention the more grim details included in what John Durham calls "as dainty and otherwise enjoyable a series of dialect stories as I have seen" (John S. Durham to CWC, May 9, 1899). A letter from Fred S. Goodman dated Nov. 3, 1899 is even more telling. He writes, "Both Mrs. Goodman and I are delighted with it. We enjoyed a pleasant evening with friends Wednesday night reading two of its chapters aloud. I think you have struck something fresh and fascinating, and have the dialect of the old time 'darkies' to a remarkable degree." Since most Chesnutt scholars agree that John and Annie were designed to embody, respectively, the skeptical and sympathetic aspects of white Northerners, it is ironic that *both* of the Goodmans appear to have "enjoyed" the book on its surface level alone.

8. Lucinda MacKethan, *The Dream of Arcady: Place and Time in Southern Literature* (Baton Rouge: Louisiana State University Press, 1980), 217. All subsequent quotations are cited parenthetically in the text.

9. Richard Brodhead, *The Journals of Charles W. Chesnutt* (Durham, NC: Duke University Press, 1993), 139-40. All subsequent quotations are cited parenthetically in the text.

10. Moreover, as Sandra Molyneaux suggests in "Expanding the Collective Memory: Charles W. Chesnutt's *The Conjure Woman* Tales," "one must be careful not to assume that Chesnutt wrote for a homogeneous Negro audience: some prosperous, educated blacks particularly in the North, dissociated themselves from rural, uneducated Blacks, a theme sparklingly dramatized in *Jelly's Last Jam*. Also, some of Chesnutt's 'cultivated' white readers would enter the dialogue and respond to the truth within. Others, like John, would not. Chesnutt wrote to them all" (175).

11. Charles Waddell Chesnutt, letter to Houghton, Mifflin & Co., 24 November 1899, Charles W. Chesnutt Papers, Fisk University Library, Nashville, Tennessee.

12. Charles Waddell Chesnutt, letter to Houghton, Mifflin & Co., 24 November 1899, Charles W. Chesnutt Papers, Fisk University Library, Nashville, Tennessee.

13. CWC, letter to Houghton, Mifflin & Co., 14 December 1899, Charles W. Chesnutt Papers, Fisk University Library, Nashville, Tennessee.

14. Richard Brodhead, *The Conjure Woman and Other Conjure Tales* (Durham, N.C.: Duke University Press, 1993), 16. All subsequent quotations are cited parenthetically in the text.

15. CWC to Albion Tourgee, dated September 26, 1889, quoted in William L. Andrews, *The Literary Career of Charles W. Chesnutt* (Baton Rouge: Louisiana State University Press, 1980), 21. All subsequent quotations are cited parenthetically in the text.

16. Michael Kreyling, "Introduction," George Washington Cable, *The Grandissimes: A Story of Creole Life* (New York: Penguin Books, 1988), vii. All subsequent quotations are cited parenthetically in the text.

17. There are several similarities between the two men's literary careers. Like Chesnutt, Cable used local color as an entree into the literary marketplace. Cable's first story, "Bibi," was about a proud African king who was enslaved and sent to Louisiana. The slave's pride leads him to resist slavery, and he is punished for that resistance. Cable was unable to find a publisher. He did, however, "learn quickly what the editor[s] wanted," and soon six "acceptable New Orleans local color stories" were collected, with an additional story, into *Old Creole Days* and published in 1879 (ix). As Kreyling writes, "If Cable had stopped [with the style of *Old Creole Days*], he would have achieved the reputation of the average Southern local colorist. . . . But he was more ambitious (ix). As for Chesnutt, Andrews writes, "The publication of these [first] four Uncle Julius stories could easily be judged as the "entering wedge" into the literary world which Chesnutt had long pointed toward in his dream of becoming a novelist. Having tested the waters of public opinion, Chesnutt could have sailed his three initial conjure stories toward greater fame as a dialectician and southern regionalist (21). Both men, it seems, could have been local colorists of note had they wished.

There are still more parallels. Cable's success came in his late thirties as he was trying to find a way leave his position on the Cotton Exchange in New Orleans to "live on his writing" (ix), in much the same way Chesnutt was trying to find a way to leave the law and live as a writer. Ultimately, the two men's eventual outcomes mirrored each other. Like Chesnutt, Cable had a brief flash with critical and popular success before his positions on race and the inevitable toll those positions took on his relationship with his audience led him to a "decline" (xiii).

18. CWC to Mrs. Alice Haldeman, February 1, 1896: "My works however are principally yet unwritten, or at least unpublished. Such fugitive pieces as I have given to the world however, have perhaps gained recognition in higher authors quarters than the productions of any other acknowledged colored writer in the United States, and have won for me the personal acquaintance and friendship of some of the most widely known literary (sic) of the country, among whom I may instance Mr. George W. Cable and Hon. A. W. Tourgée. I ought to perhaps write more and mean to do so, although of recent years my professional occupations have absorbed the greater part of my time; I am an attorney by profession and it is difficult for a man to serve two masters. . . ."

19. Sylvia Lyons Render, *The Short Fiction of Charles W. Chesnutt* (Washington D.C.: Howard University Press, 1974), 31-2. All subsequent quotations are cited parenthetically in the text.

20. There has been cursory and scattered discussion of Chesnutt's attempts to address a black audience. Andrews, in his "Color Line Stories" chapter of *The Literary Career of Charles Chesnutt*, refers to Chesnutt's "Uncle Peter's House" when he writes, "One should not conclude . . . that Chesnutt's short stories indict white people as the sole impediments to the black man's march of progress. Often the author directed his black readers to their own failure to 'finish that house' of prosperity and respectability first erected by Uncle Peter, the pioneering member of the black bourgeoisie in Chesnutt's fiction" (85).

Like Andrews, Hemenway briefly discusses Chesnutt's audience in "The Functions of Folklore in Charles Chesnutt's *The Conjure Woman*":

> No one can be completely certain how Charles Chesnutt conceived of his audience for *The Conjure Woman*, but Chesnutt was aware of the problems encountered by a black writer addressing a predominantly white 19th century reading public. . . . Chesnutt knew his books would be read by black readers . . . but only late in his life did he openly acknowledge the demands his audience had made; he told the predominantly black crowd gathered in his honor as he received the NAACP's Spingarn Award in 1928: "I had to sell my books chiefly to white readers." (302)

21. "Mars' Jeems's Nightmare" can also be read as a revision of Charles Dickens' "A Christmas Carol." In his journals Chesnutt refers to Dickens three times; he not only admired Dickens' prose, but his social commitment as well. On August 25, 1874, he talks of rereading a "splendid" *Pickwick Papers* (50). Almost a year later, on August 13, 1875, he reacts to a "splendid" *Barnaby Rudge* by writing, "I wish I could write like Dickens, but alas! I can't" (80). Six years later, in July of 1881, he writes, "I believe that, except the living example of a pure life, there is no agency so potent for leading the youthful mind to high aspirations as good books. Happy is the man who can read and appreciate the history, real or ideal, of a good man's life; and happier still is he who possesses the firmness and perseverance to carry out the good resolutions which the reading of such books always leads him to form. The writer of such a book as "David Copperfield" . . . gives to literature a *moral* force, whose effect upon the young of future generations is simply incalculable" (167 italics added). Chesnutt's admiration of Dickens' ability to fuse "splendid" writing with "moral force" is in line with his respect for Tourgée and Cable, for similar reasons.

22. SallyAnn Ferguson, "Chesnutt's 'The Conjurer's Revenge': The Economics of Direct Confrontation," *Obsidian* 7.2-3 (Summer-Winter 1981), 41. All subsequent quotations are cited parenthetically in the text.

23. Richard Baldwin, "The Art of *The Conjure Woman*," *American Literature* 43 (1971), 394.

24. Arlene Elder, *The Hindered Hand: Cultural Implications of Early African-American Fiction* (Westport, Conn: Greenwood Press, 1978), 162-3.

25. Robert Bone, *Down Home: Origins of the Afro-American Short Story* (New York: Columbia University Press, 1988), 84.

26. Eric Selinger, "Aunts, Uncles, Audience: Gender and Genre in Charles Chesnutt's *The Conjure Woman*," *Black American Literature Forum* 25.4 (Winter 1991), 665-6.

27. Indeed, as Henry Wonham points out, "rather than understand "Hot-Foot Hannibal" as an anamalous default on the subversive promise of earlier stories, like "Po' Sandy" and "Mars Jeems's Nightmare," in which Julius appears to assert a measure of creative control over his and John's environment, "Hot-Foot" should serve to qualify that promise by reminding us that Julius's narrative blend of conjure and persuasion is thoroughly and ambivalently entangled in the cultural circumstances of the postwar plantation. His capacity for resistance is always limited by his participation in a system of hierarchies that he can nudge, perhaps modify, but never escape. . . to read selectively from *The Conjure Woman* is to risk idealizing the ex-slave's powers of vernacular resistance, and thereby to obscure what emerges in a tale like "Hot-Foot Hannibal" as the unwelcome but, to Chesnutt, essential sense of Julius's limitation" (58).

28. *The Colophon* contains no pagination.

29. Frederick Douglass, *My Bondage and My Freedom*, William L. Andrews, ed., (Urbana, Ill: University of Illinois Press, 1987), 45.

30. Charles Scruggs, *Sweet Home: Invisible Cities in the Afro-American Novel* (Baltimore: The Johns Hopkins University Press, 1993), 216. All subsequent quotations are cited parenthetically in the text.

31. It is interesting that Chesnutt declined to give John and Annie last names. Certainly the omission is intentional; I believe he is cleverly commenting on the common white convention, both before and after emancipation, of enforcing and maintaining the racial hierarchy by addressing African Americans by *their* first names. This ironic reversal mandates that at least two whites will forever after be referred to by their first names as well.

32. Charles W. Chesnutt, *The Conjure Woman* (Ann Arbor: University of Michigan Press, 1969),12-13. All subsequent quotations are cited parenthetically in the text.

33. Virtually all heroines of novels written by African-American writers of the period are light-skinned. The central characters in Frances E. W. Harper's *Iola Leroy* (1892), Pauline Hopkins's *Contending Forces* (1900), and William Wells Brown's *Clotel* (1853), for example, all have very light skin, as do many of the women of the earlier slave narratives (Henry Bibb's first wife Malinda—and quite possibly his second, Mary— in *Narrative of the Life and Adventures of Henry Bibb, An American Slave, Written by Himself* [1850] ; Harriet Jacobs' Linda Brent in *Incidents in the Life of a Slave Girl* [1861], among others). Indeed, my sense is that Chesnutt didn't pointedly identify her as light-skinned because he felt he didn't need to; he assumed it would be assumed.

I will discuss the status opposition in more detail below, but the hegemonic determination of what constitutes "beauty" is certainly a part of the (cultural) white power discussed later in the chapter. Perhaps the narrator of Ann T. Greene's "The Ugly Man" puts it best: "[B]eauty is in the eye of the oppressor" (79). Also, see my own "'How come he don't like my hair?': Constructing Alternative Standards of Beauty in Toni Morrison's *Song of Solomon* and Zora Neale Hurston's *Their Eyes Were Watching God*" (*African American Review* 29.4, Winter, 1995: 579-92), for a discussion of African-American women and the European standard of beauty.

34. Chesnutt subtly mutes the details of the crossdressing episode. It is clear that (a) Hannibal dresses up to impersonate Chloe, and (b) the ruse was successful to the extent that Jeff "jump up en run to'ds dat 'oman, en th'ow his a'ms roun' her neck" (218). Conveniently, Chesnutt has Chloe quickly turn and run up to the house, since the immediate aftermath of Jeff throwing his arms around Hannibal would certainly have revealed the scheme. Absent the details, however, it is impossible to tell, for instance, whether Hannibal "lightened" his skin to the extent that he would be mistaken for Chloe, although he almost certainly did so.

35. Chesnutt did write three Uncle Julius stories between 1891 and March 30, 1898 (the day Walter Hines Page proposed a book of conjure stories, whereupon Chesnutt produced six new tales): "A Deep Sleeper," published in *Two Tales* (1893), "Lonesome Ben," submitted to and rejected by Page at the *Atlantic Monthly* (1897), and "The Dumb Witness," tentatively accepted by Page that same year. None of these three stories are "conjure" tales; while "Dave's Neckliss" was obviously not his last dialect story, he did not write another conjure story until he wrote the six that completed *The Conjure Woman*.

36. Like the "victory" of a more humane overseer (and the troubling implication that happier slaves work harder and thus make more money for their owners) in "Mars Jeems's Nightmare," this tale offers a "success" *within* the slavery system, and does not proffer freedom from slavery as the always/already primary goal. Although some of the stories deal with escape ("Po' Sandy," for example), apparently physical freedom is not the ultimate consideration.

37. While Chesnutt's transition period between 1889-1891 was legitimate, he had difficulty relating to blackness throughout his life. The letter to Houghton, Mifflin in which he refers to himself as "an American of acknowledged African descent" is a good example. Not only does he equivocate in the interest of the book's "reception by critics or the public," but the draft of the letter reveals his uneasiness with his racial identity as well. The original draft reads,

> In this case the infusion of African blood is very small, and so imperceptible that it could only be known to those who had been informed of it. But it is enough, combined with the fact that I was substantially brought up in the South, to give me a knowledge of the people I have attempted to describe. These people have never been treated from a sympathetic standpoint; they have not had their day in Court. Their friends have written of them, and their enemies; but this is, so far as I know, the first instance where one of their own blood, however small the proportion, has attempted literary portrayal of them.

The finished product, with some of the changes italicized, reads,

> In this case, the infusion of African blood is very small–*is not in fact a visible admixture*–but it is enough, combined with the fact that *the writer* was practically brought up in the South, to give *him* a knowledge of the people *whose description is attempted*. These people have never been treated from a closely sympathetic standpoint; they have not had their day in court. Their friends have written of them, and their enemies; but this is, so far as I know, the first

instance where a *writer* with any of their own blood has attempted a literary portrayal of them. (Helen Chesnutt 69)

Chesnutt clearly has difficulty openly identifying himself with blackness, as his distancing shift to third-person demonstrates. Ironically, it is this very blackness that Chesnutt feels makes his fiction especially worthy of consideration. The above paragraph ends with, "If these stories have any merit, I think it is more owing to this new point of view than to any other thing" (Helen Chesnutt 69).

38. Hurston's 1928 essay "How It Feels to Be Colored Me" demonstrates her awareness of audience as she talks of how "white people . . . liked to hear me 'speak pieces' and sing and wanted to see me dance the parse-me-la, and gave me generously of their small silver for doing these things, which seemed strange to me for I wanted to do them so much that I needed bribing to stop. Only they didn't know it. The colored people gave no dimes. They deplored any joyful tendencies in me, but I was their Zora nevertheless. I belonged to them, to the nearby hotels, to the county–everybody's Zora" (152-3). In this excerpt Hurston demonstrates her awareness of the difficulty of addressing a dual audience.

NOTES TO CHAPTER 2

1. Henry Louis Gates, Jr. *The Signifying Monkey: A Theory of African-American Literary Criticism* (New York: Oxford University Press, 1988), 185. All subsequent quotations are cited parenthetically in the text.

2. Gates describes the "mode of narration" in the novel as "narrative commentary (rendered in third-person omniscient and third-person restricted voices) and of characters' discourse (which manifests itself as a direct speech rendered in what Hurston called dialect). Hurston's innovation is to be found in the middle spaces between these two extremes of narration and discourse . . . indirect discourse and free indirect discourse." It is this innovation, he continues, "which enables her to represent various traditional modes of Afro-American rhetorical play while simultaneously representing her protagonist's growth in self-consciousness through free indirect discourse" (191). Michael Awkward, on the other hand, contends that Hurston's novel is "very much concerned with discussing the possible potency of voice and the consequences of its absence. Measuring the troublesome narration of Hurston's novel against tropes of Black expression can lead one to realize that its narrative strategies–long held to be faulty–are, rather, a stunningly successful act in the *denigration* of the novel as an expressive form" (*Inspiriting Influences: Tradition, Revision, and Afro-American Women's Novels* [New York: Columbia University Press, 1989], 48. All subsequent quotations are cited parenthetically in the text). For the purposes of this discussion, however, I agree with Hazel Carby, who feels "it is necessary to step outside questions of voice and issues of third-person (as opposed to first-person) narration in order to understand why Hurston needs an instrument of mediation between the teller of the tale and the tale itself" ("The Politics of Fiction, Anthropology, and the Folk: Zora Neale Hurston," *New Essays on* Their Eyes Were Watching God, Michael Awkward, ed. [New York: Cambridge University Press, 1990], 92n. All subsequent quotations are cited parenthetically in the text).

3. Zora Neale Hurston, *Their Eyes Are Watching God* (New York: Harper and Row, 1990), 1. All subsequent quotations are cited parenthetically in the text.

4. See Michael Awkward, "'The inaudible voice of it all': Silence, Voice, and Action in *Their Eyes Were Watching God*," in *Black Feminist Criticism and Critical Theory*, edited by Houston A. Baker, Jr. and Joe Weixlmann (Greenwood, FL: Penkevill, 1988): 57-109; Klaus Benesch, "Oral Narrative and Literary Text: Afro-American Folklore in *Their Eyes*," *Callaloo* 11.3 (Summer 1988): 627-35; Glynis Carr, "Storytelling as Bildung in Zora Neale Hurston's *Their Eyes*," *CLA Journal* 31.2 (Dec 1987): 189-200; Emily Dalgarno, "'Words Walking Without Masters': Ethnography and the Creative Process in *Their Eyes*," *American Literature* 64.3 (Sept 1992): 519-41; Henry Louis Gates, Jr., "Zora Neale Hurston and the Speakerly Text," in *The Signifying Monkey* (New York: Oxford University Press, 1988): 170-216; Barbara Johnson, "Metaphor, Metonymy, and Voice in *Their Eyes*," in *Black Literature and Literary Theory*, edited by Henry Louis Gates, Jr. (New York: Methuen, 1984): 205-21; Carla Kaplan, "The Erotics of Talk: 'That Oldest Human Longing" in *Their Eyes*," *American Literature* 67.1 (Mar 1995): 115-42; Mary O'Connor, "Zora Neale Hurston and Talking between Cultures," *Canadian Review of American Studies* (1992): 141-61; Maria J. Racine, "Voice and Interiority in Zora Neale Hurston's *Their Eyes*," *African American Review* 28.2 (Summer 1994): 283-92; Biman Basu, "'Oral Tutelage' and the Figure of Literacy: Paule Marshall's *Brown Girl, Brownstones* and Zora Neale Hurston's *Their Eyes Were Watching God*," *MELUS* 24.1 (Spring 1999): 161-76; Julie Haurykiewicz, "From Mules to Muliebrity: Speech and Silence in *Their Eyes Were Watching God*," *Southern Literary Journal* 29.2 (Spring 1997): 45-60; Maria J. Johnson, "'The World in a Jug and the Stopper in [Her] Hand': *Their Eyes Were Watching God* as Blues Performance," *African American Review* 32.3 (Fall 1998): 401-14.

5. Mary Helen Washington, "Foreword," Zora Neale Hurston, *Their Eyes Are Watching God* (New York: Harper and Row, 1990) ix.

6. Anne Pellowski, *The World of Storytelling* (Bronx, NY: H. W. Wilson Company, 1990), 17.

7. Linda Dégh, *Narratives in Society: A Performer-Centered Study of Narration* (Helsinki: Academia Scientiarum Fennica, 1995), 72. All subsequent quotations are cited parenthetically in the text.

8. Geneva Smitherman, *Talkin' and Testifyin': The Language of Black America* (Boston: Houghton Mifflin Company, 1977), 103-4. All subsequent quotations are cited parenthetically in the text.

9. Linda Goss and Mariam E. Barnes, eds., *Talk That Talk: An Anthology of African-American Storytelling* (New York: Simon and Schuester/Touchstone, 1989),10. All subsequent quotations are cited parenthetically in the text.

10. The first storytelling event of the book occurs when Nanny tells Janie her slave narrative. After slapping Janie, Nanny pulls her onto her lap, and tells her tale. Janie listens in silence. From a listener's standpoint, Janie does not come to the tale in a willing fashion, even though the information she gleans is important.

11. Missy Dehn Kubitschek, *Claiming the Heritage: African-American Women Novelists and History* (Jackson: University of Mississippi, 1991) 62. All subsequent quotations are cited parenthetically in the text.

12. The idea of a moneyed older woman blithely leaving town with a younger man and returning broke and broken is, surely, nothing new. It would be overstating the point to say that had Annie Tyler never met Who Flung the porch sitters would not have any specific reason to speculate as to why Janie was returning to Eatonville. Undoubtedly the porch-sitters would have come up with a reason to disparage Janie upon her return from the muck, even if it had meant dredging up some distant, archetypal version of the above scenario. However, the Tyler-Who Flung incident *did* happen relatively recently, and it *was* fresh in the mind of everyone in town, thereby making it a handy explanation of the return of Janie.

13. Although the narrator says Tea Cake "talked and acted out the story" (116), the narrator relates his tale, rather than expressing it in his own voice. The result is *un*like chapter two, where Nanny tells her tale in her voice, and is rather more like the novel-length, third-person tale at large. When Tea Cake returns from winning Janie's money back, however, the narrator relates a short, page-long tale of the night's events.

14. The term is Robert Stepto's. See "Distrust of the Reader in Afro-American Narratives" in *From Behind the Veil: A Study of Afro-American Narrative*, 207.

15. Pheoby refers to herself as Janie's "best friend" as early as page three of the novel, and readers are reminded of this fact on page seven ("Pheoby, we been kissin'-friends for twenty years"), page 78 ("So [Janie] went straight to her bosom friend, Pheoby Watson, and told her about it"), page 105 ("yo' buddy," says Sam Watson to wife Pheoby, "is all tied up with dat Tea Cake"), and page 106 ("But anyhow, she's yo' bosom friend, so you better go see 'bout her," Sam Watson continues). It is necessary that the narrator reminds the reader that Pheoby and Janie are best friends because even though Pheoby gives every indication that she is, ultimately, worthy of her status as Janie's "bosom friend," her connection to the porch-sitters is not nearly as peripheral as she argues that it is.

16. John Callahan, *In the African-American Grain: Call and Response in the Twentieth Century Black Fiction* (Middletown, Conn: Wesleyan University Press, 1988), 122. All subsequent quotations are cited parenthetically in the text.

17. Anita M. Vickers, "The Reaffirmation of African-American Dignity Through the Oral Tradition in Zora Neale Hurston's *Their Eyes Were Watching God*," *CLA Journal* 37.3 (Mar 1994), 314.

18. Cathy Bingham, "The Talking Frame of Zora Neale Hurston's Talking Book: Storytelling as Dialectic in *Their Eyes Were Watching God*," 419. *CLA Journal* 37.4 (June 1994), 419.

19. Elizabeth Meese, *Crossing the Double-Cross: The Practice of Feminist Criticism* (Chapel Hill, N.C.: The University of North Carolina Press, 1986), 51. All subsequent quotations are cited parenthetically in the text.

20. Zora Neale Hurston, *Mules and Men* (New York: Harper and Row, 1990), 2-3.

21. Sandra Dolby Stahl, in a section of *Literary Folkloristics and the Personal Narrative* called "Personal Narratives and the Creation of Intimacy," writes that "when people tell personal narratives, they offer their listeners an invitation to intimacy. They expect their listeners to listen because both they and their listeners know that this is one very effective (and acceptable) way to create and enjoy a sense of intimacy" ([Bloomington: Indiana University Press, 1989], 37). This intimacy is why the narrator refers to inti-

mate talk as a manner of "kissing." In the midst of disparaging the community in the open frame, Janie wonders why they can't come and sit and listen. "If they wants to see and know," she says, "why they don't come kiss and be kissed? Ah could then sit down and tell 'em things" (6).

22. Maria Tai Wolff, "Listening and Living: Reading and Experience in *Their Eyes Were Watching God*," *Black Aamerican Literature Forum* 16.1 (Spring 1982), 32.

NOTES TO CHAPTER 3

1. Ross Chambers, in *Story and Situation: Narrative Seduction and the Power of Fiction* (Mineapolis: University of Minnesota Press, 1984), defines an embedded narrative as "narrative act within narrative act, narrative situation within narrative situation: it implies the representation, internally to the fictional framework, of a situation involving the major components of a communicational act (emitter-discourse-recipient)—and very frequently the mirroring within a story of the storytelling relationship itself: narrator-narration-narratee" (33).

2. Susan Rubin Suleiman, *Authoritarian Fictions: The Ideological Novel As a Literary Genre* (New York: Columbia University Press, 1983), 65. All subsequent quotations are cited parenthetically in the text . I'm certain Ellison would object to my analyzing his novel with the assistance of a book which contains the term "Ideological Novel" in the subtitle, an objection I can certainly understand. He is quite explicit in "The World and the Jug": "I can only ask that my fiction be judged as art; if it fails, it fails aesthetically, not because I did or did not fight some ideological battle" (*The Collected Essays of Ralph Ellison*, John Callahan, editor, [New York: Modern Library, 1995], 182. All subsequent quotations are cited parenthetically in the text). "Ideology" is, to some, a fighting word. And yet, as Raymond Williams writes in *Marxism and Literature* (New York: Oxford University Press, 1985), "there is an obvious need for a general term to describe not only the products but the processes of all signification, including the signification of values" (70). Furthermore, Ellison himself, in "Society, Morality and the Novel," pretty much agrees with Williams (without using the word itself), when he writes,

It is by appealing to our sense of experience and playing upon our shared assumptions that the novelist is able to reveal to us that which we do not know—that is, the unfamiliar with the familiar—and affirm that which we assume to be the truth, and to reveal to us his own hard-won vision of the truth.

In this sense the novel is rhetorical. Whatever else it tries to do, it must do so by persuading us to accept the novelist's projection of an experience which, on some level or mixtures of levels, we have shared with him, and through which we become empathetically involved in the illusory and plotted depiction of life we identify as fictional art. (697)

3. Perhaps the most popular definition of the blues mode comes from Ellison himself:

The blues is an impulse to keep the painful details and episodes of a brutal experience alive in one's aching consciousness, to finger its jagged grain, and to transcend it, not by the consolation of philosophy but by squeezing from it a near-tragic, near-comic lyricism. As a form, the blues is an autobiographical chronicle of personal catastrophe expressed lyrically. (*Collected Essays* 129)

My contention here is that Trueblood's tale-as-blues is the model for Invisible Man's autobiography-as-blues, that the tale Trueblood tells is a crucial early step in Invisible Man's maturation into a bluesman who can, by the time he has finished his autobiography, deal with the ambivalence that grows out of the tragedy and absurdity of the Negro existence in America.

4. Houston A. Baker, Jr., describes Trueblood as a bluesman in "To Move without Moving: Creativity and Commerce in Ralph Ellison's Trueblood Episode": "The main character in the Trueblood episode ... is a country blues singer (a tenor of "crude, high, plaintively animal sounds") who is also a virtuoso prose narrator. . . . Trueblood [has a] dual manifestation as trickster and merchant, as creative and commercial man. Blues and narration, as modes of expression, conjoin and divide in harmony with these dichotomies. And the episode in its entirety is . . . a metaexpressive commentary on the incumbencies of Afro-American artists and the effects of their distinctive modes of expression" (*Blues, Ideology and Afro-American Literature: A Vernacular Theory* [Chicago: The University of Chicago Press, 1984],175. All subsequent quotations are cited parenthetically in the text). Other descriptions of Trueblood as a blues artist can be found in E.M. Kist, "A Langian Analysis of Blackness in Ralph Ellison's *Invisible Man, Studies in Black Literature* 7 (1976), 23; Raymond Olderman, "Ralph Ellison's Blues and *Invisible Man,*" *Wisconsin Studies in Contemporary Literature* 7 (1966), 146; George E. Kent, "Ralph Ellison and the Afro-American Folk and Cultural Tradition," in *Ralph Ellison: A Collection of Critical Essays.* Ed. John Hersey. Englewood Cliffs, N.J.: Prentice-Hall, 1974, 45-6; and Robert G. O'Meally, *The Craft of Ralph Ellison,* Cambridge, Mass.: Harvard University Press, 1980, 86-7; Marvin F. Thomas, "Children of Legba: Musicians at the Crossroads in Ralph Ellison's Invisible Man," *American Literature* 68:3 (Sept 1996): 587-608.

5. Ralph Ellison, *Invisible Man* (New York: Vintage Books, 1989), 3. All subsequent quotations are cited parenthetically in the text.

6. The "source" of Trueblood's difficulties are twofold. Yes, he committed incest with his daughter, but Ellison is careful to provide the reader with a context for that intercourse by revealing the economic difficulties that prompted his sleeping in the same bed with his wife and teenage daughter. By no means does that excuse the behavior, but it does allow the space to view Trueblood as a heroic figure–not, of course, for the initial action, but for extricating himself from the position in which his actions placed him.

7. Robert Stepto, "Distrust of the Reader in Afro-American Narratives." *From Behind the Veil: A Study of Afro-American Narrative.* 2nd ed. (Urbana, Ill: University of Illinois Press, 1991), 207. All subsequent quotations are cited parenthetically in the text.

8. Henry Louis Gates, Jr. "King of Cats," *The New Yorker* (8 April 1996), 76. All subsequent quotations are cited parenthetically in the text.

9. This issue of belief is an all too common one in African-American storytelling. I discuss it in detail in my sixth chapter, below.

10. Trueblood must have altered somewhat the description of the incest act, depending on the audience before him. I cannot imagine that a man as audience-aware as Trueblood would have gone into such vivid detail describing the way Matty Lou eventually "gits to movin' herself. . . [and] grabs holt to me and holds tight" (60) while trying to calm and explain to Kate what happened that morning. The idea of Trueblood actually saying to his wife, in front of his daughter, "She didn't want me to go then–and to tell the honest-to-God truth I found out that I didn't want to go neither" [60] would, it seems to me, greatly strain credulity.

11. Wolfgang Iser, *The Implied Reader: Patterns of Communication in Prose Fiction from Bunyon to Beckett.* (Baltimore: The Johns Hopkins University Press, 1974), 121. All subsequent quotations are cited parenthetically in the text.

12. Although it is easy to think of the book as existing in a linear form, it is, like *Their Eyes Were Watching God*, a circular narrative. Invisible Man writes, early in the prologue, "But that's getting too far ahead of the story, almost to the end, although the end is in the beginning and lies far ahead" (6). And in the last sentence before the epilogue, he restates, "The end was in the beginning" (571).

13. After all, as Suleiman points out, "The persuasive effect of a story of apprenticeship 'with a thesis' results from a virtual identification of the reader with the protagonist. If the protagonist evolves toward a euphoric position, the reader is incited to follow him in the right direction: the protagonists's happiness is both a proof and a guarantee of the values he affirms. If the protagonist's story 'ends badly,' his failure also serves as a lesson or proof, but this time *a contrario*: the protagonist's fate allows the reader to perceive the wrong road without following it" (73). She is saying, in essence, that where readers "live," so to speak, will determine how their identification with characters will affect them. In this particular context, it is entirely possible that while both black and white readers chiefly identify with Invisible Man, some white (and, undoubtedly, some black) readers who identified with Mr. Norton during chapter two must confront his static characterization in the epilogue.

14. Michel Fabre, "The Narrator/Narratee Relationship in *Invisible Man.*" *Callaloo* (8.3 Fall, 1985), 535. All subsequent quotations are cited parenthetically in the text.

15. John S. Wright, "The Conscious Hero and the Rites of Man: Ellison's War," *New Essays on* Invisible Man, Robert O'Meally, editor (Cambridge, Mass.: Cambridge University Press, 1988), 176.

NOTES TO CHAPTER 4

1. James Alan McPherson, "The Story of a Scar," *Elbow Room* (Boston : Little, Brown, 1977), 79. All subsequent quotations are cited parenthetically in the text.

2. Orlando Patterson, *Rituals of Blood: Consequences of Slavery in Two American Centuries* (New York: Basic Civitas, 1998), x. All subsequent quotations are cited parenthetically in the text.

3. Robert Stepto, "Distrust of the Reader in Afro-American Narratives," *From Behind the Veil: A Study of Afro-American Narrative* (Urbana, Ill: University of Illinois Press, 1991), 198. All subsequent quotations are cited parenthetically in the text.

4. Patricia Hill Collins, *Black Feminist Thought: Knowledge, Consciousness, and the Politics of Empowerment* (New York: Routledge, 1991), 183. All subsequent quotations are cited parenthetically in the text.

5. John's skepticism and Annie's empathy inform their ways of listening to Uncle Julius's tales in Charles W. Chesnutt's *The Conjure Woman* (Ann Arbor: The University of Michigan Press, 1969), particularly at the end of "Po' Sandy" (60-62); Phoebe's early belief that Tea Cake has abandoned Janie (7) influences her response to Janie's tale in Zora Neale Hurston's *Their Eyes Were Watching God* (New York: Harper and Row, 1990; all subsequent quotations are cited parenthetically in the text); and the title character's black middle class pretensions (46-7)–to say nothing of Mr. Norton's relationship with his late daughter (43)–each color their respective reactions to Jim Trueblood's tale in *Invisible Man* (New York: Vintage Books, 1989). These assumptions, when made an explicit part of the storytelling event, can heighten the teller's sense of distrust.

6. "Largely provided by European anthropological discourses emerging with imperialism," writes Collins in *Fighting Words: Black Women and the Search for Justice* (Minneapolis: University of Minnesota Press, 1998), "the notion of Blacks as primitive helped establish a logic for understanding Africa and peoples of African descent. Black people in so-called primitive societies were increasingly cast as more natural, sexual, and primitive than Whites or others touched by the civilizing influences of European culture. Moreover, the emergence of a racist biology that linked inferiority with immutable biological differences meant that the stigma of race was seen as intergenerational and permanent. Africans carried the primitive's mark of immutable difference with them wherever they went" (99).

7. Jon Wallace, "The Politics of Style in Three Stories by James Alan McPherson," *Modern Fiction Studies* 34 (Spring 1988), 17-18. All subsequent quotations are cited parenthetically in the text.

8. The dozens is a form of "Signifyin(g)," itself a black discursive "mode of figuration," writes Henry Louis Gates, Jr. in *The Signifying Monkey: A Theory of African-American Literary Criticism* (New York: Oxford University Press, 1988). "The black rhetorical tropes, subsumed under Signifyin(g), would include marking, loud-talking, testifying, calling out (of one's name), sounding, rapping, playing the dozens, and so on" (52). The dozens "is perhaps the best-known mode of Signification, both because it depends so heavily on humor and because the success of its exchanges turns on insults of one's family members, especially one's mother" (99).

9. This tension between the individual and the collective highlights what Ralph Ellison calls the "cruel contradiction" at the heart of the African-American vernacular tradition. The group creation mode is implicit in oral communication (i.e., a speaker needs listeners). This black vernacular group mode is evident in everything from sermonizing to rap freestyling, and the individual-improvising-with-and-against-the-collective impulse has existed from the ancient Ring Shout to the modern Soul Train line. Ellison, writing specifically about jazz in "The Charlie Christian Story" in *The Collected Essays of Ralph Ellison* (John F. Callahan, ed., New York: The Modern Library, 1995), offers a wonderful description of the high stakes for an improviser in a group setting:

> [T]rue jazz is an art of individual assertion within and against the group.
> Each true jazz moment . . . springs from a contest in which each artist chal-
> lenges all the rest; each solo flight, or improvisation, represents (like the suc-
> cessive canvases of a painter) a definition of his identity as an individual, as
> member of the collectivity and as a link in the chain of tradition. Thus,
> because jazz finds its very life in an endless improvisation upon traditional
> materials, the jazzman must lose his identity even as he finds it. . . . (267)

Red Bone's grandmother, then, comments on the underlying tension inherent in group
creation, and clearly stands on conformity. Billy Crawford, obviously, relishes his non-
conformity, and it is the tension between the two—with the scarred woman caught in
the middle—that drives the teller's tale.

  10. The scarred woman's allusion to "the grapevine" reveals yet another form of
vernacular orality. Referred to as "the wire" (97) in *The Autobiography of Malcolm X*
(New York: Ballantine Books, 1973) and present, by various names, in countless other
texts, this mode of oral communication transfers information from one person to
another by "word of mouth." Indeed, Red Bone, as well, says to the teller above, "*People
sayin'* you been wearing a high hat since you started goin' with the professor. *The talk
is* you been throwin' around big words. . .*" (103, emphasis mine). Interestingly, a comparison of these two excerpts demonstrates how references to the oral informational
networks alone—given that the teller was included in the one that discussed Teddy
Johnson and excluded from the one Red Bone had access to—mark the factionalization
among the postal employees.

  11. The teller refers to the "bad nigger" archetype here. As Lawrence W. Levine
writes in *Black Culture and Black Consciousness: Afro-American Folk Thought From Slavery
To Freedom* (New York: Oxford University Press, 1977), "From the late nineteenth century black lore was filled with tales, toasts, and songs of hard, merciless toughs and
killers confronting and generally vanquishing their adversaries without hesitation and
without remorse" (407-8). Levine adds,

> One of the most recent creations in this genre, the Great MacDaddy, whose
> story Roger Abrahams encountered in Philadelphia during the 1950s,
> remains wholly within the tradition. Arrested and brought to trial, his bad-
> ness impresses even the judge who tells him: "You're the last of the bad. /
> Now Dillinger, Slick Willie Sutton, all them fellows is gone, / Left you, the
> Great MacDaddy to carry on." Although he treats his sister-in-law and
> mother-in-law with contempt, they pass him two guns which enable him to
> escape. Finally he is shot in the back by a policeman, but to the end he typ-
> ifies the totally hard man:
>
> I've got a tombstone disposition, a graveyard mind.
>
> I know I'm a bad motherfucker, that's why I don't mind dying. (413)

Ultimately, Levine argues—in terms that the narrator of "A Story of a Scar" doesn't
seem to understand–, "Black singers, storytellers, and audiences might temporarily and
vicariously live through the exploits of their bandit heroes, but they were not beguiled
into looking to these asocial, self-centered, and futile figures for any permanent reme-
dies. . . ." African-Americans did, however, appreciate a "hero who by transcending

society's restrictions and stereotypes could directly confront it on its own terms and emerge victorious" (420).

12. Recall that before Janie Starks left Eatonville with a handsome, younger man named Tea Cake, Annie Tyler, also "a widow with a good home and insurance money" (113), left Eatonville with a handsome, younger man named Who Flung. Two weeks after they left, Tyler returned, having been abandoned by Who Flung. This Tyler-Who Flung narrative is alluded to by the porch-sitters as Janie walks into town to open the novel (2), recalled by Janie when Tea Cake leaves her alone in their hotel room overnight (113-15), and is in Pheoby's mind as she sits down to listen to Janie's story (7).

13. For a well-rounded discussion of the way "cool" functions in African-American culture, see Richard Majors and Janet Mancini Billson's *Cool Pose: The Dilemmas of Black Manhood in America* (New York: Lexington Books, 1992), especially chapters two and five.

14. Michele Wallace, *Black Macho and the Myth of the Superwoman* (New York: Verso, 1990), 23-4. All subsequent quotations are cited parenthetically in the text.

15. Joseph T. Cox, "James Alan McPherson," *Contemporary Fiction Writers of the South* (Westport, Conn: Greenwood Press, 1993), 315.

16. Herman Beavers, "'I Yam What You Is and You Is What I Yam: Rhetorical Invisibility in James Alan McPherson's 'The Story of a Dead Man,'" *Callaloo* 9 (fall, 1986): 367.

NOTES TO CHAPTER 5

1. Ralph Ellison, *The Collected Essays of Ralph Ellison,* John Callahan, editor (New York: Modern Library, 1995), 344. All subsequent quotations are cited in the text.

2. Houston A. Baker, Jr., *Blues, Ideology, and Afro-American Literature* (Chicago: The University of Chicago Press, 1984),13. All subsequent quotations are cited in the text.

3. David Levering Lewis, *When Harlem Was in Vogue* (New York: Oxford University Press, 1981), 171. All subsequent quotations are cited in the text.

4. Toni Morrison's *Jazz* (New York: Alfred A. Knopf, 1992) is, in that sense, well-named. Her novel set in 1926 Harlem combines the southern blues aesthetic with a northern jazz reality, including a folk narrator who states unequivocally, "I love this City" (7) and describes it for several pages.

5. Toni Cade Bambara, "My Man Bovanne," *Gorilla, My Love* (New York: Vintage Books, 1981), 4. All subsequent quotations are cited in the text.

6. The "formal rebellion" that I compare to the civil rights movement operates on more than one level. In much the same way African-Americans have struggled for freedom and independence from white domination in one way or another since we were brought here, the aforementioned timeline makes it clear that African-American writers have periodically constructed spoken-voice narratives with no interior listeners well before the 1960s. But "the sixties" (a term that generally includes the fifties' wind-up and the seventies' wind-down) are known for being a time when the struggle was more energized (if not more organized) and gained a higher profile than in earlier eras.

And the corresponding creative activity was also a time that, while not technically "new" was noteworthy and energetic as well.

In that sense, terms such as "formal rebellion" do not refer to the formal "newness" of the period in the sense that it had never been done before. It is more akin to what Geneva Smitherman writes in *Talkin and Testifyin: The Language of Black America* (Boston: Houghton Mifflin Company, 1977):

> Within the limitations of written form, today's poets are attempting to capture the flavor of Black American speech–its rhythms and sounds, its dialect and style. They use Black English not only to project the voice of a black character in a poem, but even when they are speaking in their own poetic voices in a given poem. Through their artistic efforts, the poets seem to be saying: if the message is new, the medium must be new also. (180)

Even if the form isn't truly "new" at all.

7. Raymond Hedin, in "Probable Readers, Possible Stories: The Limits of Nineteenth-Century Black Narrative" (*Readers in History: Nineteenth-Century American Literature and the Contexts of Response*, James L. Machor, editor [Baltimore: The Johns Hopkins University Press, 1993]. All subsequent quotations are cited in the text), touches on the way *power* relationships, issues of agency and autonomy, drove frame use as early as *The Confessions of Nat Turner* (1831), Douglass's "The Heroic Slave," Chesnutt's *The Conjure Woman*, and Sutton Griggs's *Imperium in Imperio* (1899). Hedin suggests that it was only when blacks "began to write again with an angry voice that they again sought mediation–and faced again the issues of voice and presence inherent in such mediation" (191). Although Hedin's "angry voice" theory has merit, throughout American literature writers have felt that the colloquial black voice, angry or otherwise, must be contained in order to placate the American readership. Hedin suggests, for example, that *The Conjure Woman* had to "pass" in order to pass muster: "Becoming fit to survive often involved the narrative equivalent of 'passing,' with similarly inherent ambiguities. The black story had to look like a white story; it had to at least look like a story which was fully acceptable to the whites who heard it inside the text" (195).

8. Hoyt W. Fuller, "The New Black Literature: Protest or Affirmation," *The Black Aesthetic*, Addison Gayle, Jr., editor (Garden City, New York: Doubleday & Company, 1971), 351-2.

9. Raymond Hedin, "Probable Readers, Possible Stories: The Limits of Nineteenth-Century Black Narrative," *Readers in History: Nineteenth-Century American Literature and the Contexts of Response*, James L. Machor, editor (Baltimore: The Johns Hopkins University Press, 1993), 198. All subsequent quotations are cited in the text.

10. Toni Cade Bambara, *Deep Sightings and Rescue Missions: Fiction, Essays, and Conversations*, Toni Morrison, editor (New York: Pantheon Books, 1996), 48.

11. See introduction.

12. Zora Neale Hurston, *Their Eyes Were Watching God* (New York: Harper and Row, 1990), 183.

13. Houston Baker's after-the-fact discussion of the Black Aesthetic helps delineate the movement's goals and aims. Baker explains, in *Blues, Ideology, and Afro-American Literature*, that "traditional white, critical orthodoxy" that was "repudiated by a Black

Aesthetic generation was the customary faith that sustained the idea of AMERICA. The sole basis for privileging the standards of a white, literary-critical establishment was the faith that this establishment's values and practices were instrumental in a dauntless progress toward AMERICA. The Black Aesthetic generation realized that the cost of such a faith was an ironic and unpluralistic relinquishing of one's own particularity ('structural' or otherwise) in the service of a pluralistic immanent idea. Their realization led to a declaration of heterodoxy" (83).

Perhaps more importantly, Baker explains the source of the Black Aesthetics' sense of black authenticity when he argues, "The distinctive cultural circumstances that comprised the material bases of Afro-American culture–the 'economics of slavery'–were always seen by spokesmen for the Black Aesthetic as determinants of a distinctively 'black' consciousness. And the most accurate reflection of the economics of slavery (and their subsequent forms) in the American economy was held to take place at a mass or vernacular level. Hence, the expressive forms of black folk consciousness were defined by Black Aestheticians as underdetermined by material circumstances that were held to vary within a narrow range. To take up such forms, therefore, according to Black Aestheticians, is perforce, to find oneself involved with the *authentic* or *basic* (as in the 'material base') categories of Afro-American existence" (84).

Baker does point out that there were "blatant weaknesses in the theoretical framework of the Black Aesthetic. Too often in attempts to locate the parameters of Afro-American culture, Black Aesthetic spokesmen settled instead for romantically conceived boundaries of 'race'" (84-5). Baker does find it "encouraging, however, in an evaluation of the Afro-American intellectual milieu that prevailed during the later stages of the Black Arts movement, that Black Aesthetic spokesmen *themselves* were the first to point out (and to suggest ways beyond) the critical and theoretical weaknesses of their new paradigm"(85).

14. Julian Mayfield, "You Touch My Black Aesthetic and I'll Touch Yours," *The Black Aesthetic,* Addison Gayle, Jr., editor (Garden City, New York: Doubleday & Company, 1971), 24.

15. Larry Neal, *Visions of a Liberated Future: Black Arts Movement Writings* (New York: Thunder's Mouth Press, 1989), 63.

16. James T. Stewart, *The Black Aesthetic,* Addison Gayle, Jr., editor (Garden City, New York: Doubleday & Company, 1971), 348.

17. In "The Myth of the Black Matriarchy" (*The Black Scholar* [Jan-Feb 1990], Robert Staples argues that the liberation struggle "must be cognizant of the need to avoid a diffusion of energy devoted to the liberation struggle lest it dilute the over-all effectiveness of the movement. Black women cannot be free qua women until all blacks attain their liberation" (15-16). Black women in the sixties were divided on the matter. Some women agreed with Staples's position, while others attempted to pursue both liberation struggles at the same time.

Kathleen Cleaver provides an example of how tenuous the latter position could be: "[I]n order to resolve that problem between the black man and the black woman, the whole system of colonialism must first be destroyed. . . . This is where the liberation of women becomes so crucial. That as long as the men deny the women their full role and their full respect in that struggle . . . they are cutting themselves short and they're selling the struggle short" (Julia Herve, "*Black Scholar* Interviews Kathleen Cleaver," *The Black Scholar* [Dec 1991], 59). Cleaver argues for the respect and "liberation" of women so that the revolution can be hastened and yet somehow insists that before the black male/black female problem can be "resolved," the system must be felled. Many women in the movement executed just this sort of rhetorical balancing act as they tried to avoid, in Staples's terms, "diluting" and "hindering" the struggle while still agitating for respect and an increased role in political decisions.

18. Toni Cade Bambara, editor, *The Black Woman: An Anthology* (New York: New American Library, 1970), 7. All subsequent quotations are cited in the text.

19. Alice Walker, *In Love and Trouble: Stories of Black Women* (New York: Harcourt Brace Jovanovich, 1973), 57. All subsequent quotations are cited in the text.

20. The two stories also share a brief discussion of black hair as a window on intra-black relations. The narrator describes Dee (Wangero) as having hair that "stands straight up like the wool on a sheep. It is black as night and around the edges are two long pigtails that rope about like small lizards disappearing behind her ears." Dee's male companion is described as having hair "all over his head a foot long and hanging from his chin like a kinky mule tail" (52). The hair meshes with the Swahili greeting, the recently-acquired African name, and the new attitude toward her rural past as Dee's attempt to completely redefine her upbringing. Similarly, at one point in "My Man Bovanne," daughter Elo points to Hazel's wig and asks, "Is your hair braided up under that thing? If so, why don't you take it off? You always did a neat cornroll." Hazel takes the opportunity to say, "'Uh huh,' cause I'm thinking how she couldn't undo her hair fast enough talking bout cornroll so countrified" (7). Each story's hair references speak not only to the difficulty of adapting to rapidly-changing "approved" modes of black expression, but also to the tension between rural "folk" vs. "acceptable" urban modes of blackness, and to the way they change in relation to how this or that generation of African-Americans feel about themselves.

21. Gayl Jones, *Liberating Voices: Oral Tradition in African-American Literature* (Cambridge: Harvard University Press, 1991), 137.

22. See this study's introduction, above, for a discussion of Walter Ong's "audience readjustment" question.

23. Gerald Prince, "Introduction to the Study of the Narratee," *Reader-Response Criticism: From Formalism to Post-Structuralism,* Jane P. Tompkins, editor (Baltimore: The Johns Hopkins University Press, 1980), 19. All subsequent quotations are cited in the text. In Bambara's case, the narratee is a listener (the "'you,'" in a text, writes Prince, "is the narratee" [9]). Since, as Prince argues, the narratee is "always part of the narrative framework" (22), he or she "can, thus, exercise an entire series of functions in a narra-tive: he constitutes a relay between the narrator and the reader, he helps establish the narrative framework, he serves to characterize the narrator, he emphasizes certain themes, he contributes to the development of the plot, he becomes the spokesman for the moral of the work" (23). Additionally, Prince alludes to frame texts when he dis-cusses the placement of a narratee in the text as a character: The narratee is "often of a particularly concrete framework in which the narrator(s) and the narratee(s) are all characters (*Heart of Darkness, L'Immoraliste, The Decameron*). The effect is to make the

narrative seem more natural. The narratee like the narrator plays an undeniable *versimilating (vraisemblabilisant)* [sic] role" (22).

24. Jane Tompkins, "An Introduction to Reader-Response Criticism," *Reader-Response Criticism: From Formalism to Post-Structuralism* (Baltimore: The Johns Hopkins University Press, 1980), xii.

25. Robert Stepto, "Distrust of the Reader in Afro-American Narratives," *From Behind the Veil: A Study of Afro-American Narrative*, 2nd edition (Urbana, Ill: University of Illinois Press, 1991), 204.

26. In the introduction to the collection of essays he edited, *The Black Aesthetic*, Addison Gayle chides "the Aristotelian Critics, the Practical Critics, the Formalist Critics, and the New Critics" for their aim "to evaluate the work of art in terms of *its* beauty and not in terms of the transformation from ugliness to beauty that the work of art demands from its audience." He adds, "A critical methodology has no relevance to the black community unless it aids men in becoming better than they are. . . . The Black Aesthetic, then, as conceived by this writer, is a corrective–a means of helping black people out of the polluted mainstream of Americanism. . . . To be an American writer is to be an American, and, for black people, there should no longer be honor attached to either position" (xxii).

27. Certainly, black texts have white readers as well as black. Stepto addresses this fact in his "Afterword":

> Once we acknowledge . . . that nonframed Afro-American tales also assume a white readership, we may say that, in their narrative intentions and recognition of communicative prospects, both types of written tales are far more candid than the reader-response literary critics have been about how acts of listening and reading may be complicated by race. (205)

This complication, however, does not happen at the level of narrative in stories such as "My Man Bovanne." Mama Hazel's narratee is black and female, and although white readers might respond differently than black readers, when the virtual reader is black, the *intent* of the author is not complicated by race in the same way other stories with different narrators and narratees would be.

28. Larry Neal, *Visions of a Liberated Future: Black Arts Movement Writings* (New York: Thunder's Mouth Press, 1989), 77-8. All subsequent quotations are cited in the text.

29. The fact that these are Mama Hazel's biological children who insist that she alter her behavior in no way diminishes the story's metaphorical allusion to the Black Aesthetician's relationship to black writers who operated outside of the parameters of the Black Arts Movement. In fact, it enhances the allusion since, during the sixties and seventies, it became more fashionable than ever for blacks to refer to each other as "brother" and "sister," as in, say, last chapter's text, James Alan McPherson's "The Story of A Scar" (1977), makes clear. Bambara has made the perfect choice by painting a critique of the Black Aesthetic as familial concern. After all, Bambara does give Hazel and her children the family name "Peoples."

30. See special section on Ellison in *Callaloo* 18.2 (1995): 249-320, and "Robert Hayden and Michael S. Harper: A Literary Friendship" (ed. Xaiver Nicholas) in

Callaloo 17.4 (1994): 976-979, for some examples of the difficulty these writers experienced during the sixties era.

31. Charles Johnson, *Being and Race* (Bloomington: Indiana University, 1988), 19-27; Trey Ellis, "The New Black Aesthetic," *Callaloo* (12.1 1989), 236.

32. Toni Cade Bambara, "Black Woman/Black Man: Closer Together or Further Apart? . . .Compared to What?" *Essence* (Oct 1973), 37.

33. In *Time* magazine's cover story, "The Beauty of Black Art," Jack E. White writes that recent books by Maya Angelou, the Delany sisters, and Nathan McCall all "attracted a large number of both white and black readers" (69). White also quotes Charles Harris, then president and publisher of New York City's Amistad Press, as saying, "We've laid to rest the racist canard in the publishing industry that black people don't read" (69-70). Henry Louis Gates, in an accompanying essay, adds, "the rise of a black middle class has provided for black art a market that is independent of whites" (75). And Bebe Moore Campbell, in a *USA Today* article called, "Black Authors Celebrate their Growing Visibility" says, "Publishers discovered they had been leaving money on the table" by not recognizing there was a market for books by black authors. Campbell went on to call 1992 the "defining year" for black literature sales (5D).

(A short corrective of sorts was published in the Washington *Post* on April 5, 1996. Writers such as Ishmael Reed, Amiri Baraka and Eugene Redmond "argued that an increase in black books from major publishing houses does not constitute a African-American literary renaissance like those of the 1920s and 1960s" [F2]. On one level, this disagreement is no different than, say, Sterling Brown's disagreement with the idea of a Negro Renaissance, or the ideological battles of the sixties. Taken a different way, however, these writers could be pointing out the false dichotomy between the business of publishing and the art of fiction. Another possibility is that *any* sense that this time is in any way analogous to the Harlem Renaissance or the Black Arts Movement is threatening to those who have an investment in the previous movements. Regardless of whether their opposition stems from one or all of the above, the dissent is very real.)

NOTES TO CHAPTER 6

1. Robert Stepto, "Distrust of the Reader in Afro-American Narratives," *From Behind the Veil: A Study of Afro-American Narrative*, 2nd ed, (Urbana, Ill: University of Illinois Press, 1991), 198. All subsequent quotations are cited in the text.

2. John Edgar Wideman, "Doc's Story," *Fever: Twelve Stories* (New York: Penguin Books, 1989), 11. All subsequent quotations are cited in the text.

3. John Edgar Wideman, *Philadelphia Fire* (New York: Vintage Contemporaries, 1990), 40. All subsequent quotations are cited in the text.

4. This problem certainly can be experienced by some blacks, as well. When I call this a cultural setting, I don't mean to imply that all blacks can immediately experience communal audience pleasure merely because of the color of their skin.

5. Nelson George, *Elevating the Game: Black Men and Basketball* (New York: HarperCollins, 1992), xv.

6. Arthur Ashe, *A Hard Road to Glory: The African-American Athlete in Basketball* (New York: Amistad, 1993), 24.

7. Ralph Ellison, *The Collected Essays of Ralph Ellison*, John Callahan, editor (New York: Modern Library, 1995), 344.

8. The discourse of distrust has a long history. As Stepto writes, "While it was Douglass's audience's distrust of him that led to the *Narrative* [of 1845], it was his increasing distrust of *them* that prompted *My Bondage* [*and My Freedom*] as well as his newspapers, his novella, "The Heroic Slave," and his removal, in fine American form, to the "West" (Rochester, N.Y.). In short, the illiteracy of the allegedly literate spurred Douglass the speaker to become also Douglass the writer and editor" (196). "The Heroic Slave" is one of the earliest African-American storytelling texts, and the written-storytelling arm of the discourse of distrust was born with the frame-text form itself.

9. Chesnutt W. Chesnutt, *The Conjure Woman* (Ann Arbor: University of Michigan Press, 1969), 107. All subsequent quotations are cited in the text.

10. Kimberly W. Benston, editor, *Speaking for You: The Vision of Ralph Ellison* (Washington, D.C.: Howard University Press, 1987), 120.

11. Lawrence Levine, *Black Culture and Black Consciousness: Afro-American Folk Thought from Slavery to Freedom* (New York: Oxford University Press, 1977), x-xi.

12. Rayford Logan, *The Negro in American Life and Thought: the Nadir, 1877-1901* (New York: Dial Press, 1954), 52.

13. Ralph Ellison, *Invisible Man* (New York: Vintage Books, 1989), 52-3.

14. Stepto describes Type B' stories as follows "(a) although the story's primary narrator is a novice teller (white or black), the black master teller is fully present as the teller of the story's tale; (b) although the novice teller may tell the tale of his or her previous incompetency to listeners situated within the tale's frame, direct address to the 'listener' outside the story (the 'outside' reader) is both possible and likely; (c) although the predominating autobiographical statement is still that offered by the master teller in the tale, the novice teller's self-history also has a place, sometimes a significant one, in the story as a whole; (d) although the story is normally a frame tale, with this type we begin to see improvisations upon that structure, especially in those instances where the story is repeated and otherwise developed for the needs and purposes of novellas and novels" (209).

Bibliography

Andrews, William L. *The Literary Career of Charles W. Chesnutt.* Baton Rouge: Louisiana State University Press, 1980.

_____. "The Novelization of Voice in Early African American Narrative." *PMLA* (Jan 1990, 105.1): 23-34.

Ashe, Arthur. *A Hard Road to Glory: The African-American Athlete in Basketball.* New York: Amistad, 1993.

Awkward, Michael. Inspiriting Influences: Tradition, Revision, and Afro-American Women's Novels. New York: Columbia University Press, 1989.

_____, ed. *New Essays on* Their Eyes Were Watching God. Cambridge: Cambridge University Press, 1990.

Baker, Houston A., Jr. *Blues, Ideology, and Afro-American Literature: A Vernacular Theory.* Chicago: The University of Chicago Press, 1984.

_____. *Long Black Song: Essays in Black American Literature and Culture.* Charlottesville: The University Press of Virginia, 1990.

Baldwin, Richard E. "The Art of *The Conjure Woman.*" *American Literature* 43 (1971): 385-98.

Bambara, Toni Cade, ed. *The Black Woman: An Anthology.* New York: New American Library, 1970.

_____. "Black Woman/Black Man: Closer Together or Further Apart? . . . Compared to What?" *Essence* (Oct 1973): 37+.

_____. *Deep Sightings and Rescue Missions: Fiction, Essays, and Conversations*. Ed. Toni Morrison. New York: Pantheon Books, 1996.

_____. *Gorilla, My Love*. New York: Vintage Books, 1981.

Baraka, Amiri (LeRoi Jones). *Blues People*. William Morrow & Company, 1983.

Beavers, Herman. "'I Yam What You Is and You Is What I Yam: Rhetorical Invisibility in James Alan McPherson's 'The Story of a Dead Man.'" *Callaloo* 9.4 Fall 1986: 565-77.

Benston, Kimberly W., ed. *Speaking for You: The Vision of Ralph Ellison*. Washington, D.C.: Howard University Press, 1987.

Bingham, Cathy. "The Talking Frame of Zora Neale Hurston's Talking Book: Storytelling as Dialectic in *Their Eyes Were Watching God*." *CLA Journal*. (37.4, June 1994): 402-19.

Bone, Robert. *Down Home: Origins of the Afro-American Short Story*. New York: Columbia University Press, 1988.

Bradley, David. *The Chaneysville Incident*. New York: Harper and Row, 1981.

Britt, David D. "Chesnutt's Conjure Tales: What You See Is What You Get," *CLA Journal* 15.3 (March, 1972): 269-83.

Brodhead, Richard H., ed. "Introduction." *The Conjure Woman and Other Conjure Tales*. Durham, N.C.: Duke University Press, 1993.

_____. *Cultures of Letters: Scenes of Reading and Writing in Nineteenth-Century America*. Chicago: University of Chicago Press, 1993.

_____. *The Journals of Charles W. Chesnutt*. Durham, N.C.: Duke University Press, 1993.

Burroway, Janet. *Writing Fiction: A Guide to Narrative Craft*. New York: HarperCollins, 1987.

Cable, George Washington. *The Grandissimes: A Story of Creole Life*. New York: Penguin Books, 1988.

Callahan, John F. In the African-American Grain: Call and Response in Twentieth-Century Black Fiction. Middletown, Conn.: Wesleyan University Press, 1988.

Carby, Hazel V. "The Politics of Fiction, Anthropology, and the Folk: Zora Neale Hurston." *New Essays on* Their Eyes Were Watching God. Ed. Michael Awkward. New York: Cambridge University Press, 1990.

Chambers, Ross. *Story and Situation: Narrative Seduction and the Power of Fiction.* Minneapolis: University of Minnesota Press, 1984.

Chesnutt, Charles W. *The Conjure Woman.* Ann Arbor: University of Michigan Press, 1969.

_____. "Post-Bellum–Pre-Harlem," *The Colophon: A Book Collector's Quarterly.* (Part Five, 1931): no pagination.

Chesnutt, Helen M. *Charles Waddell Chesnutt: Pioneer of the Color Line.* Chapel Hill: University of North Carolina Press, 1952.

Collins, Patricia Hill. *Black Feminist Thought: Knowledge, Consciousness, and the Politics of Empowerment.* New York: Routledge, 1991.

_____. *Fighting Words: Black Women and the Search for Justice.* Minneapolis: University of Minnesota Press, 1998.

Cox, Joseph T. "James Alan McPherson," *Contemporary Fiction Writers of the South.* Westport, Conn: Greenwood Press, 1993

Dégh, Linda. Narratives in Society: A Performer-Centered Study of Narration. Helsinki: Academia Scientiarum Fennica, 1995.

Douglass, Frederick. *My Bondage and My Freedom.* Ed. William L. Andrews. Urbana and Chicago: University of Illinois Press, 1987.

DuBois, W.E.B. *The Souls of Black Folks.* New York: Bantam Books, 1989.

Dunbar, Paul Laurence. "The Race Question." *The Heart of Happy Hollow.* Dodd, Mead, 1904.

Edwards, Viv and Thomas J. Sienkewicz. *Oral Cultures Past and Present.* Cambridge, Ma: Basil Blackwell, Inc., 1991.

Elder, Arlene A. *The Hindered Hand: Cultural Implications of Early African-American Fiction.* Westport, Conn: Greenwood Press, 1978.

Ellis, Trey. "The New Black Aesthetic," *Callaloo* (12.1 1989): 236.

Ellison, Ralph. *The Collected Essays of Ralph Ellison.* John Callahan, ed. New York: Modern Library, 1995.

_____. *Invisible Man.* New York: Vintage Books, 1989.

Fabre, Geneviéve and Robert O'Meally, ed. *History and Memory in African-American Culture.* New York: Oxford University Press, 1994.

Fabre, Michel. "The Narrator/Narratee Relationship in *Invisible Man. Callaloo* (8.3 Fall, 1985): 535-43.

Ferguson, SallyAnn H. "Chesnutt's 'The Conjurer's Revenge': The Economics of Direct Confrontation." *Obsidian* 7.2-3 (Summer-Winter 1981): 37-42.

Fuller, Hoyt W. "The New Black Literature: Protest or Affirmation." *The Black Aesthetic.* Addison Gayle, Jr., ed. Garden City, New York: Doubleday & Company, 1971.

Gaines, Ernest. *The Autobiography of Miss Jane Pittman.* New York: Dial Press, 1971.

Gates, Henry Louis, Jr. "Black Creativity: On the Cutting Edge." *Time* (10 Oct 94): 74-5.

_____. and Sieglinde Lemke. "Introduction." *The Complete Stories by Zora Neale Hurston.* New York: HarperCollins, 1995.

_____. "King of Cats." *The New Yorker* 8 April 1996: 70-81.

_____. And Nellie McKay. *The Norton Anthology of African American Literature.* W. W. Norton and Company, 1997.

_____. *The Signifying Monkey: A Theory of African-American Literary Criticism.* New York: Oxford University Press, 1988.

_____. "Introduction." *The Autobiography of an Ex-Coloured Man.* James Weldon Johnson. New York: Vintage Books, 1989.

Gayle, Addison, Jr., ed. *The Black Aesthetic.* Garden City, New York: Doubleday & Company, 1971.

George, Nelson. *Elevating the Game.* New York: HarperCollins, 1992.

Gleason, William. "Chesnutt's Piazza Tales: Architecture, Race, and Memory in the Conjure Stories." *American Quarterly* 51.1 (March 1999): 33-77.

Goss, Linda and Marian E. Barnes, eds. *Talk That Talk: An Anthology of African-American Storytelling.* New York: Simon and Schuster/Touchstone, 1989.

Greene, Ann T. "The Ugly Man." *Callaloo* 12.1 (Winter, 1989): 79.

Harris, Joel Chandler. *Uncle Remus: His Songs and Sayings.* Ed. Robert Hemenway. New York: Penguin Books, 1982.

Hedin, Raymond. "Probable Readers, Possible Stories: The Limits of Nineteenth-Century Black Narrative." *Readers in History: Nineteenth-Century American Literature and the Contexts of Response*. Ed. James L. Machor. Baltimore: The Johns Hopkins University Press, 1993. 180-205.

Hemenway, Robert. "The Functions of Folklore in Charles Chesnutt's *The Conjure Woman*." *Journal of the Folklore Institute* 13.3 (1976): 283-309.

Herve, Julia. "*Black Scholar* Interviews Kathleen Cleaver." *The Black Scholar* (Dec 1971): 54-9.

Hurston, Zora Neale. *Dust Tracks on a Road*. New York: Harper and Row, 1991.

_____. "How It Feels to Be Colored Me." *The Norton Anthology of African American Literature*. W. W. Norton & Company, 1997. 1008-11.

_____. *Mules and Men*. New York: Harper and Row, 1990.

_____. *Their Eyes Were Watching God*. New York: Harper and Row, 1990.

Iser, Wolfgang. *The Implied Reader: Patterns of Communication in Prose Fiction from Bunyon to Beckett*. Baltimore: The Johns Hopkins University Press, 1974.

Johnson, Charles. *Being and Race*. Bloomington: Indiana University, 1988.

Johnson, James Weldon. *The Autobiography of an Ex-Coloured Man*. Vintage Books, 1989.

_____. "The Dilemma of the Negro Author." *American Mercury* 15 (Dec 1928): 477-481.

Jones, Gayl. *Liberating Voices: Oral Tradition in African-American Literature*. Cambridge: Harvard University Press, 1991.

Kreyling, Michael. "Introduction." George Washington Cables, *The Grandissimes*. New York: Penguin Books, 1988.

Kubitschek, Missy Dehn. *Claiming the Heritage: African-American Women Novelists and History*. Jackson: University Press of Mississippi, 1991.

Levine, Lawrence W. *Black Culture and Black Consciousness: Afro-American Folk Thought from Slavery to Freedom*. Oxford: Oxford University Press, 1977.

Lewis, David Levering. *When Harlem Was in Vogue*. New York: Oxford University Press, 1981.

Logan, Rayford. *The Negro in American Life and Thought: the Nadir, 1877-1901.* New York: Dial Press, 1954.

MacKethan, Lucinda. *The Dream of Arcady: Place and Time in Southern Literature* Baton Rouge: Louisiana State University Press, 1980.

Maierhofer, Roberta. "Bambara's 'My Man Bovanne.'" *The Explicator* 57.1 (Fall 1998): 57-9.

Majors, Richard and Janet Mancini Billson. *Cool Pose: The Dilemmas of Black Manhood in America.* New York: Lexington Books, 1992.

Mayfield, Julian. "You Touch My Black Aesthetic and I'll Touch Yours." *The Black Aesthetic.* Addison Gayle, Jr., ed. Garden City, New York: Doubleday & Company, 1971.

McKnight, Reginald. *Moustapha's Eclipse.* New York: Ecco Press, 1989.

McMillan, Terry, ed. *Breaking Ice: An Anthology of Contemporary African-American Fiction.* New York: Penguin Books, 1990.

McPherson, James Alan. "Indivisible Man." *The Collected Essays of Ralph Ellison.* John Callahan, ed. New York: Modern Library, 1995. 353-95.

_____. *Elbow Room.* Boston : Little, Brown, 1977

Meese, Elizabeth A. *Crossing the Double-Cross: The Practice of Feminist Criticism.* Chapel Hill, N.C.: The University of North Carolina Press, 1986.

Molyneaux, Sandra. "Expanding the Collective Memory: Charles W. Chesnutt's *The Conjure Woman* Tales." *Memory, Narrative, and Identity: New Essays in Ethnic American Literatures.* Amritjit Singh, Joseph T. Skerrett, Jr., Robert E. Hogan, eds. Boston: Northeastern University Press, 1994.

Morrison, Toni. *Jazz.* New York: Alfred A. Knopf, 1992.

Naylor, Gloria. *Mama Day.* New York: Ticknor & Fields, 1988.

Neal, Larry. *Visions of a Liberated Future: Black Arts Movement Writings.* New York: Thunder's Mouth Press, 1989.

Ong, S.J. Walter J. *Interfaces of the Word: Studies in the Evolution of Consciousness and Culture.* Ithaca, N.Y.: Cornel University Press, 1977.

Patterson, Orlando. *Rituals of Blood: Consequences of Slavery in Two American Centuries.* New York: Basic Civitas, 1998.

Page, Thomas Nelson. *In Ole Virginia; Or, Marse Chan and Other Stories,* 1892.

Pearson, John H. "The Politics of Framing in the Late Nineteenth Century." *Mosaic* 23.1: 15-30.

Pellowski, Anne. *The World of Storytelling.* Bronx, NY: The H.W. Wilson Company, 1990.

Prince, Gerald. "Introduction to the Study of the Narratee." *Reader-Response Criticism: From Formalism to Post-Structuralism.* Ed. Jane P. Tompkins. Baltimore: The Johns Hopkins University Press, 1980.

Render, Sylvia Lyons, ed. *The Short Fiction of Charles W. Chesnutt.* Washington, D.C.: Howard University Press, 1974.

Rubin, Louis D. Jr. *The History of Southern Literature.* Baton Rouge: Louisiana State Press, 1985.

Salaam, Kalamn ya. "Searching for the Mother Tongue." *First World* 2.4 (1980): 48-53.

Scruggs, Charles. *Sweet Home: Invisible Cities in the Afro-American Novel.* Baltimore: The Johns Hopkins University Press, 1993.

Selinger, Eric. "Aunts, Uncles, Audience: Gender and Genre in Charles Chesnutt's *The Conjure Woman.*" *Black American Literature Forum* 25.4 (Winter 1991): 665-88.

Skaggs, Merrill Maguire. *The Folk of Southern Fiction.* Athens: The University of Georgia Press, 1972.

Smitherman, Geneva. *Talkin and Testifyin: The Language of Black America.* Boston: Houghton Mifflin Company, 1977.

Stahl, Sandra Dolby. *Literary Folkloristics and the Personal Narrative.* Bloomington: Indiana University Press, 1989.

Staples, Robert. "The Myth of the Black Matriarchy," *The Black Scholar* (Jan.-Feb., 1970): 8-16.

Stepto, Robert B. "Distrust of the Reader in Afro-American Narratives." *From Behind the Veil: A Study of Afro-American Narrative.* 2nd ed. Urbana, Ill: University of Illinois Press, 1991. 195-215.

_____. *From Behind the Veil: A Study of Afro-American Narrative.* 2nd ed. Urbana, IL: University of Illinois Press, 1991.

Suleiman, Susan Rubin. *Authoritarian Fictions: The Ideological Novel As a Literary Genre.* New York: Columbia University Press, 1983.

Tompkins, Jane P., ed. "An Introduction to Reader-Response Criticism." *Reader-Response Criticism: From Formalism to Post-Structuralism.* Baltimore: The Johns Hopkins University Press, 1980.

Tolliver, Melba. "Black Authors Celebrate their Growing Visibility." *USA Today* (26 Mar 96): 5D.

Vickers, Anita M. "The Reaffirmation of African-American Dignity Through the Oral Tradition in Zora Neale Hurston's *Their Eyes Were Watching God.*" *CLA Journal.* (37.3, Mar 1994): 303-15.

Wainwright, Mary Katherine. "The Aesthetics of Community: The Insular Black Community as Theme and Focus in Hurston's *Their Eyes Were Watching God.*" *The Harlem Renaissance: Reevaluations.* Eds. Armitjit Singh, William S. Shiver, Stanley Brodwin. New York: Garland Publishing, Inc., 1989.

Walker, Alice. *In Love and Trouble: Stories of Black Women.* New York: Harcourt Brace Jovanovich, 1973.

Wallace, Jon. "The Politics of Style in Three Stories by James Alan McPherson." *Modern Fiction Studies* 34.1 Spring 1988: 17-26.

Wallace, Michele. *Black Macho and the Myth of the Superwoman.* New York: Verso, 1990.

Washington, Mary Helen. "Foreword." *Their Eyes Were Watching God.* New York: Harper and Row, 1990. vii-xiv.

White, Jack E. "The Beauty of Black Art." *Time* (10 Oct 94): 67-73.

Wideman, John Edgar. *Fever: Twelve Stories.* New York: Penguin Books, 1989.

_____. "Frame and Dialect: The Evolution of the Black Voice in American Literature." *The American Poetry Review* (Sept-Oct 1976): 34-7.

_____. *Philadelphia Fire.* New York: Vintage Contemporaries, 1990.

Williams, Raymond. *Marxism and Literature.* Oxford: Oxford University Press, 1985

Wolff, Maria Tai. "Listening and Living: Reading and Experience in *Their Eyes Were Watching God,*" *Black American Literature Forum* 16.1 (Spr 1982): 29-33.

Wonham, Henry B. "'The Curious Psychological Spectical of a Mind Enslaved': Charles W. Chesnutt and Dialect Fiction." *Mississippi Quarterly* 51:1 (1997-98): 55-69

Wright, John S. "The Conscious Hero and the Rites of Man: Ellison's War." *New Essays on* Invisible Man. Ed. Robert O'Meally. Cambridge, Mass.: Cambridge University Press, 1988.

X, Malcolm. *The Autobiography of Malcolm X.* New York: Ballantine Books, 1973.

Index

A

Ashe, Arthur, *A Hard Road to Glory*, 98
Andrews, William L., 10
    on publishing history of *The Conjure
        Woman*, 14
    on "Hot-Foot Hannibal," 17
Atlanta Monthly, 1
    Aldrich, Thomas Bailey, editor of, 12
    short stories published in, 15
Awkward, Michael, 41–2, 117n

B

Baker, Houston A., Jr., 50, 51, 58, 77, 85,
        127n
Baldwin, James, 83
Baldwin, Richard, 11, 111n
Bambara, Toni Cade, 8, 62, 83
    The Black Woman, 82
    "My Man Bovanne," 3, 4, 7, 74, 77,
        80–91, 93
        and audience models, 80–2, 87
        as "frameless" storytelling event,
            79, 80
        and Gerald Prince's narrator/narratee
            theory, 79
        kitchen conference in, 86–8
        narrative negotiations in, 84, 87–90
Baraka, Amiri, *Blues People*, 110n, 130n
Beavers, Herman, 73

Bibb, Henry, 15n
Bingham, Cathy, 41
The Black Aesthetic, 81, 129n
Black Aestheticians, 81
    black artists reactions to, 89
    defined, 126–27n
    views toward African-American art,
        85–88
    as virtual reader of "My Man
        Bovanne," 84–85
The Black Scholar, 62, 127–28n
Bone, Robert, 10, 17, 111n
Britt, David, 112n
Brodhead, Richard, 10
    as editor of *The Conjure Woman and
        Other Conjure Tales*, 14
Brooks, Gwendolyn, 89
Brown, William Wells, *Clotel*, 115n

C

Cable, George Washington, 15–16, 113n
    The Grandissimes, 16
Callahan, John, 38, 39, 40, 44
Campbell, Bebe Moore, 130n
Carby, Hazel, 42, 117n
Chambers, Ross, *Story and Situation*,
        109n, 120n
The Chaneysville Incident, 99, 106
Chaucer, *The Canterbury Tales*, 5

Chesnutt, Charles Waddell, 7, 8, 29, 62, 93
  "An Inside View of the Negro Question," 15
  and black audience, 11–14, 114n
  "The Conjurer's Revenge," 14, 18, 105
  The Conjure Woman, 4, 6, 9–27, 47, 78
    publishing history of, 14–17
  "Dave's Neckliss," 14, 19
  and double audience, 9–12
  fictionalizing his audience, 10–11
  frame, use of, 10, 26. *See also* frame texts
  "The Grey Wolf's Ha'nt," 26
  "The Goophered Grapevine," 1, 13, 14, 15, 19
  "Hot-Foot Hannibal," 6, 17–27, 50
    Aunt Peggy's roots in, 20
    black power vs. white power in, 22, 24
    house/field opposition in, 21
    status vs. non-status in, 20–1, 24
  journal entries, 11–13
  "Mars Jeems' Nightmare," 17, 25
  The Marrow of Tradition, 12
  and Plantation Tradition, 10–11, 16
  "Po' Sandy," 14, 15, 19
  and racial mixture, 9, 116–17n
  and racial outlook transition period, 14–27
  "Sis' Becky's Pickaninny," 17
  "Tobe's Tribulations," 16, 19
  "What is a White Man?," 15
  The Wife of His Youth, 12, 14, 20
Helen Chesnutt, 15
Cleaver, Kathleen, 127–28n
Collins, Patricia Hill, 63, 71, 123n
The Conjure Woman. See Charles Waddell Chesnutt
Conrad, Joseph, *Heart of Darkness*, 2
Cooper, J. California, "The Life You Life (May Not Be Your Own)," 5
Cox, Joseph T., 73
Crouch, Stanley, 89

D
Dégh, Linda
  on personal narratives, 31, 43. *See also* storytelling
Dickens, Charles, 114n
Douglass, Frederick
  "The Heroic Slave," 44, 78, 99
  My Bondage and My Freedom, 19
Dove, Rita, "The Vibraphone," 5
DuBois, W. E. B.
  and double consciousness, 1, 9
  and the color line, 9
  The Souls of Black Folk, 111n
Dunbar, Paul Laurence, 7

E
Elder, Arlene, 17
Ellington, Duke, 78
Ellis, Trey, 89
Ellison, Ralph, 8, 30, 45, 77, 78. *See also Invisible Man*
  as target of Black Aestheticians, 88, 89
  "Change the Joke and Slip the Yoke," 104
  "Society, Morality and the Novel," 120n
  "Working Notes for *Invisible Man*," 48–9, 52, 53, 58

F
Fabre, Geneviéve, 1–2
Fabre, Michel, 57
Ferguson, Sally Ann, 17
Frame texts
  authorial control in, 4
  defined, 1, 2
  embedded narratives in, 2
    defined, 47
  "frameless" spoken-voice narratives in, 4, 79, 80, 91
  and "frame-smashing" of the 1960s, 78–9, 91
  and implied audience, 80, 81

and virtual frame text, 84–5
as mediating force, 11
narrative negotiations in, 1, 7, 63, 84
Chesnutt's use of, 26–7
narrative/narratee theory in, 7
significant historical, 110n
Fuller, Hoyt, 79–80, 81

G
Gaines, Ernest, 83
*The Autobiography of Miss Jane
Pittman*, 106
Gates, Henry Louis, Jr., 29, 30, 35, 42–3,
49, 55
Gayle, Addison, 129n. *See also The
Black Aesthetic*
George, Nelson, *Elevating the Game*,
98–9
Gleason, William, 111n

H
Harper, Frances, E. W., *Iola Leroy*, 115n
Harper, Michael, 89
Harris, Joel Chandler, 2, 7
Hayden, Robert, 88, 89
Hedin, Raylong, 79, 80, 126n
Hemenway, Robert, 11, 111n, 114n
Henderson, Fletcher, 77–8
Hopkins, Pauline, *Contending Forces*,
115n
Howells, William Dean, 11
Hurston, Zora Neale, 8, 47, 62. *See also
Their Eyes Were Watching God*
critiquing her audience, 30, 44–46
Dust Tracks on a Road, 42
"How It Feels to be Colored Me,"
117n
Mules and Men, 42

I
Invisible Man, 2, 3, 4, 30, 62, 78, 93, 100,
105–06
Trueblood Episode in, 47–59, 62
as "adventure," 48

the blues in, 6–7, 120–21n
Jim Trueblood in, 6, 45
as listening model, 7
as bluesman, 48–9, 77
as master storyteller, 49, 51
Mr. Norton in, 47, 52
Iser, Wolfgang, 52

J
Johnson, Charles, 89
Johnson, James Weldon, *The
Autobiography of an Ex-
Coloured Man*, 3, 80
"The Dilemma of the Negro Author,"
9, 10, 27
Jones, Gayl, 4, 83

K
Kent, George, 104
Kubitschek, Missy Dehn, 35, 42

L
Levine, Lawrence, *Black Culture and
Black Consciousness*, 104–05,
124–25n
Lewis, David Levering, 77–8
Logan, Rayford, 105

M
MacKethan, Lucinda, 11, 111n
Marshall, Paule, 89
"Reena," 78
Mayfield, Julian, 81
McKnight, Reginald, 3–4, 99
McMillan, Terry, *Waiting to Exhale*, 74
McPherson, James Alan, 8, 55
"The Story of a Scar," 4, 7, 62–75, 78,
93, 99
"cool" style in , 69–70
listening competency in, 66–72, 74
literacy and orality in, 65–69,
72–73, 74
narrative negotiations in, 63, 74
storytelling time in, 64

Meese, Elixabeth, 41, 45
Molyneaux, Sandra, 112n

N
Naylor, Gloria, *Mama Day*, 3

O
O'Meally, Robert G., 1–2
Ong, Walter, S.J., 40, 45, 48, 83, 90
    on "fictionalizing audience," 4–6

P
Page, Thomas Nelson, 2, 7
    "Marse Chan," 17
Page, Walter Hines, 18
Patterson, Orlando
    crisis in African-American gender
        relations, 61, 62–3, 74
    on "cool" style, 69
Pearson, John, 109n
Pellowski, Anne, 30
Plantation Tradition, 10, 11, 16
Prince, Gerald
    and narrator/narrator theory, 7, 83–4,
        128–29n. *See also* Bambara,
        Toni Cade

R
Randall, Dudley, 89
Redmond Eugene, 130n
Reed, Ishmael
Render, Sylvia Lyons, 10, 16

S
Scruggs, Charles
    and the "invisible city," 19
Selenger, Eric, 17
Shange, Ntozake, 61–2, 83
Shelley, Mary, *Frankenstein*, 2
Skaggs, Merrill Maguire, 111–12n
Smitherman, Geneva, *Talkin' and
        Testifyin'. See also* vernacular
    tradition
    black dialect in, 3

group norms vs. storytelling in, 31
"formal rebellion" of the 1960s in,
    126n
Sutherland, Ellease, 83
The Souls of Black Folk. See DuBois, W.
    E. B.
Spoken voice, African American, 3–4.
    See also Smitherman, Geneva
    tension between narrative frame and,
    8
Stahl, Sandra Dolby, *Literary Folkloristics
    and the Personal Narrative*,
    119–20n
Stables, Robert, 127n
Stepto, Robert, 49, 84, 96, 99, 129n,
    131n
    and authorial control, 4
    and "discourse of distrust," 7, 62, 106,
        131n
    defined, 93–4
    From Behind the Veil, 35
Steward, James T., 81
Storytelling
    aesthetic of, defined, 30–5
    and audience pleasure, 96
    as event, defined, 2
    as personal narrative, 31, 119–20n
    setting in, 98
    time in, 64
    therapeutic aspects of, 95
Suleiman, Susan Subin
    story of apprenticeship 47–8, 49,
        120n, 122n

T
*Talk That Talk: An Anthology of African-
    American Storytelling*, 31–2,
    42–3
Their Eyes Were Watching God, 4, 6,
    29–46, 47, 48, 62, 78, 80, 93
    discussion of audience, 41–2
    Janie Crawford
        as storyteller, 30
        and acquisition of storytelling
            aesthetic, 40, 42

Joe Starks
    disrupting Janie's storytelling, 33,
        34
    Pheoby Watson as listener, 6, 29–30,
        38–41, 44–6, 48, 71
    Tea Cake
        encouraging Janie's storytelling, 34
    Tyler-Who Flung narrative, 35–38,
        69, 71, 119n, 125n
    defined, 36–7
Tompkins, Jane, 84
Tourgée, Albion, 14, 113n
Twain, Mark, 2

U
Uncle Remus, 11

V
Vernacular Tradition, African American,
        31, 68, 123–24n, 124n
Vickers, Anita

W
Walker, Alice
    The Color Purple, 74
    "Everyday Use," 82
        as commentary on the Civil Rights
            Movement, 82–3
        and black hair, 128n
Wallace, Jon, 65, 66, 73
Wallace, Michele, 61–2, 71
Washington, Mary Helen, 30
White, Jack E. 130n
Wideman, John Edgar, 8, 89, 91
    on black spoken voice, 4
    "Doc's Story," 1, 4, 7, 94–107
        acquisition of listening competency
            in, 96
        blindness, 101
            girlfriend's cultural blindness,
                101
        "discourse of distrust" in, 7, 94,
            102, 103. *See also* Stepto,
            Robert

    and interrogation of frame text
        model, 106. *See also* frame
        texts
    storytelling setting in, 98
    signifyin(g) in, defined, 123n
    on *The Conjure Woman*, 102–05
    skeptical (potential) listener in, 94
    on frame texts, 11
    Philadelphia Fire, 95–6, 99
Williams, Raymond, *Marxism and
        Literature*, 120n
Williams, Sherley Anne, 3
Wolff, Maria Tai, 45
Wonham, Henry, 115n
Wright, John S., 58